Baddeck and That Sort of Thing

Charles Dudley Warner

Contents

BADDECK AND THAT

SORT OF THING

by

Charles Dudley Warner

PREFACE
TO JOSEPH H. TWICHELL

IT would be unfair to hold you responsible for these light sketches of a summer trip, which are now gathered into this little volume in response to the usual demand in such cases; yet you cannot escape altogether. For it was you who first taught me to say the name Baddeck; it was you who showed me its position on the map, and a seductive letter from a home missionary on Cape Breton Island, in relation to the abundance of trout and salmon in his field of labor. That missionary, you may remember, we never found, nor did we see his tackle; but I have no reason to believe that he does not enjoy good fishing in the right season. You understand the duties of a home missionary much better than I do, and you know whether he would be likely to let a couple of strangers into the best part of his preserve.

But I am free to admit that after our expedition was started you speedily relieved yourself of all responsibility for it, and turned it over to your comrade with a profound geographical indifference; you would as readily have gone to Baddeck by Nova Zembla as by Nova Scotia. The flight over the latter island was, you knew, however, no part of our original plan, and you were not obliged to take any interest in it. You know that our design was to slip rapidly down, by the back way of Northumberland Sound, to the Bras d'Or, and spend a week fishing there; and that the greater part of this journey here imperfectly described is not really ours, but was put upon us by fate and by the peculiar arrangement of provincial travel.

It would have been easy after our return to have made up from libraries a most engaging description of the Provinces, mixing it with historical, legendary, botanical, geographical, and ethnological information, and seasoning it with adventure from your glowing imagination. But it seemed to me that it would be a more honest contribution if our account contained only what we saw, in our rapid travel; for I have a theory that any addition to the great body of print, however insignificant it may be, has a value in proportion to its originality and individuality,--however slight either is,--and very little value if it is a compilation of the observations of others. In this case I know how slight the value is; and I can only hope that as the trip was very entertaining to us, the record of it may not be wholly unentertaining to those of like tastes.

Of one thing, my dear friend, I am certain: if the readers of this little journey could have during its persual the companionship that the writer had when it was made, they would think it altogether delightful. There is no pleasure comparable to that of going about the world, in pleasant weather, with a good comrade, if the mind is distracted neither by care, nor ambition, nor the greed of gain. The delight there is in seeing things, without any hope of pecuniary profit from them! We certainly enjoyed that inward peace which the philosopher associates with the absence of desire for money. For, as Plato says in the Phaedo, "whence come wars and fightings and factions? whence but from the body and the lusts of the body? For wars are occasioned by the love of money." So also are the majority of the anxieties of life. We left these behind when we went into the Provinces with no design of acquiring anything there. I hope it may be my fortune to travel further with you in this fair world, under similar circumstances.

NOOK FARM, HARTFORD, April 10, 1874.

C. D. W.

BADDECK AND THAT SORT OF THING

I

"Ay, now I am in Arden: the more fool I; when I was at home,
I was in a better place; but travellers must be content."

--TOUCHSTONE.

Two comrades and travelers, who sought a better country than the United States in the month of August, found themselves one evening in apparent possession of the ancient town of Boston.

The shops were closed at early candle-light; the fashionable inhabitants had retired into the country, or into the second-story-back, of their princely residences, and even an air of tender gloom settled upon the Common. The streets were almost empty, and one passed into the burnt district, where the scarred ruins and the uplifting piles of new brick and stone spread abroad under the flooding light of a full moon like another Pompeii, without any increase in his feeling of tranquil seclusion. Even the news-offices had put up their shutters, and a confiding stranger could nowhere buy a guide-book to help his wandering feet about the reposeful city, or to show him how to get out of it. There was, to be sure, a cheerful tinkle of horse-car bells in the air, and in the creeping vehicles which created this levity of sound were a few lonesome passengers on their way to Scollay's Square; but the two travelers, not having well-regulated minds, had no desire to go there. What would have become of Boston if the great fire had reached this sacred point of pilgrimage no merely human mind can imagine. Without it, I suppose the horse-cars would go continually round and round, never stopping, until the cars fell away piecemeal on the track, and the horses collapsed into a mere mass of bones and harness, and the brown-covered books from the Public Library, in the hands of the fading virgins who carried them, had accumulated fines to an incalculable amount.

Boston, notwithstanding its partial destruction by fire, is still a good place to start from. When one meditates an excursion into an unknown and perhaps perilous land, where the flag will not protect him and the greenback will only partially support him, he likes to steady and tranquilize his mind by a peaceful halt and a serene start. So we--for the intelligent reader has already identified us with the two travelers resolved to spend the last night, before beginning our journey, in the quiet of a Boston hotel. Some people go into the country for quiet: we knew better. The country is no place for sleep. The general absence of sound which prevails at night is only a sort of background which brings out more vividly the special and unexpected disturbances which are suddenly sprung upon the restless listener. There are a thousand pokerish noises that no one can account for, which excite the nerves to acute watchfulness.

It is still early, and one is beginning to be lulled by the frogs and the crickets, when the faint rattle of a drum is heard,--just a few preliminary taps. But the soul takes alarm, and well it may, for a roll follows, and then a rub-a-dub-dub, and the farmer's boy who is handling the sticks and pounding the distended skin in a neighboring horse-shed begins to pour out his patriotism in that unending repetition of rub-a-dub-dub which is supposed to represent love of country in the young. When the boy is tired out and quits the field, the faithful watch-dog opens out upon the stilly night. He is the guardian of his master's slumbers. The howls of the faithful creature are answered by barks and yelps from all the farmhouses for a mile around, and exceedingly poor barking it usually is, until all the serenity of the night is torn to shreds. This is, however, only the opening of the orchestra. The cocks wake up if there is the faintest moonshine and begin an antiphonal service between responsive barn-yards. It is not the clear clarion of chanticleer that is heard in the morn of English poetry, but a harsh chorus of cracked voices, hoarse and abortive attempts, squawks of young experimenters, and some indescribable thing besides, for I believe even the hens crow in these days. Distracting as all this is, however, happy is the man who does not hear a goat lamenting in the night. The goat is the most exasperating of the animal creation. He cries like a deserted baby, but he does it without any regularity. One can accustom himself to any expression of suffering that is regular. The annoyance of the goat is in the dreadful waiting for the uncertain sound of the next wavering bleat. It is the fearful expectation of that, mingled with the faint hope that the last was the last, that aggravates the tossing listener until he has murder in his heart. He longs for daylight, hoping that the voices of the night will then cease, and that sleep will come with the blessed morning. But he has forgotten the birds, who at the first streak of gray in the east have assembled in the trees near his chamber-window, and keep up for an hour the most rasping dissonance,--an orchestra in which each artist is tuning his instrument, setting it in a different key and to play a different tune: each bird recalls a different tune, and none sings "Annie Laurie,"--to pervert Bayard Taylor's song.

Give us the quiet of a city on the night before a journey. As we mounted skyward in our hotel, and went to bed in a serene altitude, we congratulated ourselves upon a reposeful night. It began well. But as we sank into the first doze, we were startled by a sudden crash. Was it an earthquake, or another fire? Were the neighboring buildings all tumbling in upon us, or had a bomb fallen into the neighboring crockery-store? It was the suddenness of the onset that startled us, for we soon perceived that it began with the clash of cymbals, the pounding of drums, and the blaring of dreadful brass. It was somebody's idea of music. It opened without warning. The men composing the band of brass must have stolen silently into the alley about the sleeping hotel, and burst into the clamor of a rattling quickstep, on purpose. The horrible sound thus suddenly let loose had no chance of escape; it bounded back from wall to wall, like the clapping of boards in a tunnel, rattling windows and stunning all cars, in a vain attempt to get out over the roofs. But such music does not go up. What could have been the intention of this assault we could not conjecture. It was a time of profound peace through the country; we had ordered no spontaneous serenade, if it was a serenade. Perhaps the Boston bands have that habit of going into an alley and disciplining their nerves by letting out a tune too big for the alley, and taking the shock of its reverberation. It may be well enough for the band, but many a poor sinner in the hotel that night must have thought the judgment day had sprung upon him. Perhaps the band had some remorse, for by and by it leaked out of the alley, in humble, apologetic retreat, as if somebody had thrown something at it from the sixth-story window, softly breathing as it retired the notes of "Fair Harvard."

The band had scarcely departed for some other haunt of slumber and weariness, when the notes of singing floated up that prolific alley, like the sweet tenor voice of one bewailing the prohibitory movement; and for an hour or more a succession of young bacchanals, who were evidently wandering about in search of the Maine Law, lifted up their voices in song. Boston seems to be full of good singers; but they will ruin their voices by this night exercise, and so the city will cease to be attractive to travelers who would like to sleep there. But this entertainment did not last the night out.

It stopped just before the hotel porter began to come around to rouse the travelers who had said the night before that they wanted to be awakened. In all well-regulated hotels this process begins at two o'clock and keeps up till seven. If the porter is at all faithful, he wakes up everybody in the house; if he is a shirk, he only rouses the wrong people. We treated the pounding of the porter on our door with silent contempt. At the next door he had better luck. Pound, pound. An angry voice, "What do you want?"

"Time to take the train, sir."

"Not going to take any train."

"Ain't your name Smith?"

"Yes."

"Well, Smith"--

"I left no order to be called." (Indistinct grumbling from Smith's room.)

Porter is heard shuffling slowly off down the passage. In a little while he returns to Smith's door, evidently not satisfied in his mind. Rap, rap, rap!

"Well, what now?"

"What's your initials? A. T.; clear out!"

And the porter shambles away again in his slippers, grumbling something about a mistake. The idea of waking a man up in the middle of the night to ask him his "initials" was ridiculous enough to banish sleep for another hour. A person named Smith, when he travels, should leave his initials outside the door with his boots.

Refreshed by this reposeful night, and eager to exchange the stagnation of the shore for the tumult of the ocean, we departed next morning for Baddeck by the most direct route. This we found, by diligent study of fascinating prospectuses of travel, to be by the boats of the International Steamship Company; and when, at eight o'clock in the morning, we stepped aboard one of them from Commercial Wharf, we felt that half our journey and the most perplexing part of it was accomplished. We had put ourselves upon a great line of travel, and had only to resign ourselves to its flow in order to reach the desired haven. The agent at the wharf assured us that it was not necessary to buy through tickets to Baddeck,--he spoke of it as if it were as easy a place to find as Swampscott,--it was a conspicuous name on the cards of the company, we should go right on from St. John without difficulty. The easy familiarity of this official with Baddeck, in short, made us ashamed to exhibit any anxiety about its situation or the means of approach to it. Subsequent experience led us to believe that the only man in the world, out of Baddeck, who knew anything about it lives in Boston, and sells tickets to it, or rather towards it.

There is no moment of delight in any pilgrimage like the beginning of it, when the traveler is settled simply as to his destination, and commits himself to his unknown fate and all the anticipations of adventure before him. We experienced this pleasure as we ascended to the deck of the steamboat and snuffed the fresh air of Boston Harbor. What a beautiful harbor it is, everybody says, with its irregularly indented shores and its islands. Being strangers, we want to know the names of the islands, and to have Fort Warren, which has a national reputation, pointed out. As usual on a steamboat, no one is certain about the names, and the little geographical knowledge we have is soon hopelessly confused. We make out South Boston very plainly: a tourist is looking at its warehouses through his opera-glass, and telling his boy about a recent fire there. We find out afterwards that it was East Boston. We pass to the stern of the boat for a last look at Boston itself; and while there we have the pleasure of showing inquirers the Monument and the State House. We do this with easy familiarity; but where there are so many tall factory chimneys, it is not so easy to point out the Monument as one may think.

The day is simply delicious, when we get away from the unozoned air of the land. The sky is cloudless, and the water sparkles like the top of a glass of champagne. We intend by and by to sit down and look at it for half a day, basking in the sunshine and pleasing ourselves with the shifting and dancing of the waves. Now we are busy running about from side to side to see the islands, Governor's, Castle,

Long, Deer, and the others. When, at length, we find Fort Warren, it is not nearly so grim and gloomy as we had expected, and is rather a pleasure-place than a prison in appearance. We are conscious, however, of a patriotic emotion as we pass its green turf and peeping guns. Leaving on our right Lovell's Island and the Great and Outer Brewster, we stand away north along the jagged Massachusetts shore. These outer islands look cold and wind-swept even in summer, and have a hardness of outline which is very far from the aspect of summer isles in summer seas. They are too low and bare for beauty, and all the coast is of the most retiring and humble description. Nature makes some compensation for this lowness by an eccentricity of indentation which looks very picturesque on the map, and sometimes striking, as where Lynn stretches out a slender arm with knobby Nahant at the end, like a New Zealand war club. We sit and watch this shore as we glide by with a placid delight. Its curves and low promontories are getting to be speckled with villages and dwellings, like the shores of the Bay of Naples; we see the white spires, the summer cottages of wealth, the brown farmhouses with an occasional orchard, the gleam of a white beach, and now and then the flag of some many-piazzaed hotel. The sunlight is the glory of it all; it must have quite another attraction--that of melancholy--under a gray sky and with a lead-colored water foreground.

There was not much on the steamboat to distract our attention from the study of physical geography. All the fashionable travelers had gone on the previous boat or were waiting for the next one. The passengers were mostly people who belonged in the Provinces and had the listless provincial air, with a Boston commercial traveler or two, and a few gentlemen from the republic of Ireland, dressed in their uncomfortable Sunday clothes. If any accident should happen to the boat, it was doubtful if there were persons on board who could draw up and pass the proper resolutions of thanks to the officers. I heard one of these Irish gentlemen, whose satin vest was insufficient to repress the mountainous protuberance of his shirt-bosom, enlightening an admiring friend as to his idiosyncrasies. It appeared that he was that sort of a man that, if a man wanted anything of him, he had only to speak for it "wunst;" and that one of his peculiarities was an instant response of the deltoid muscle to the brain, though he did not express it in that language. He went on to explain to his auditor that he was so constituted physically that whenever he saw a fight, no matter whose property it was, he lost all control of himself. This sort of confidence poured out to a single friend, in a retired place on the guard of the boat, in an unexcited tone, was evidence of the man's simplicity and sincerity. The very act of traveling, I have noticed, seems to open a man's heart, so that he will impart to a chance acquaintance his losses, his diseases, his table preferences, his disappointments in love or in politics, and his most secret hopes. One sees everywhere this beautiful human trait, this craving for sympathy. There was the old lady, in the antique bonnet and plain cotton gloves, who got aboard the express train at a way-station on the Connecticut River Road. She wanted to go, let us say, to Peak's Four Corners. It seemed that the train did not usually stop there, but it appeared afterwards that the obliging conductor had told her to get aboard and he would let her off at Peak's. When she stepped into the car, in a flustered condition, carrying her large bandbox, she began to ask all the passengers, in turn, if this was the right train, and if it stopped at Peak's. The information she received was various, but the weight of it was discouraging, and some of the passengers urged her to get off without delay, before the train should start. The poor woman got off, and pretty soon came back again, sent by the conductor; but her mind was not settled, for she repeated her questions to every person who passed her seat, and their answers still more discomposed her. "Sit perfectly still," said the conductor, when he came by. "You must get out and wait for a way train," said the passengers, who knew. In this confusion, the train moved off, just as the old lady had about made up her mind to quit the car, when her distraction was completed by the discovery that her hair trunk was not on board. She saw it standing on the open platform, as we passed, and after one look of terror, and a dash at the window, she subsided into her seat, grasping her bandbox, with a vacant look of utter despair. Fate now seemed to have done its worst, and she was resigned to it. I am sure it was no mere curiosity, but a desire to be of service, that led me to approach her and say, "Madam, where are you going?"

"The Lord only knows," was the utterly candid response; but then, forgetting everything in her last misfortune and impelled to a burst of confidence, she began to tell me her troubles. She informed me that her youngest daughter was about to be married, and that all her wedding-clothes and all her summer clothes were in that trunk; and as she said this she gave a glance out of the window as if she hoped it might be following her. What would become of them all now, all brand new, she did n't know, nor what would become of her or her daughter. And then she told me, article by article and piece by piece, all that that trunk contained, the very names of which had an unfamiliar sound in a railway-car, and how many sets and pairs there were of each. It seemed to be a relief to the old lady to make public this catalogue which filled all her mind; and there was a pathos in the revelation that I cannot convey in words. And though I am compelled, by way of illustration, to give this incident, no bribery or torture shall ever extract from me a statement of the contents of that hair trunk.

We were now passing Nahant, and we should have seen Longfellow's cottage and the waves beating on the rocks before it, if we had been near enough. As it was, we could only faintly distinguish the headland and note the white beach of Lynn. The fact is, that in travel one is almost as much dependent upon imagination and memory as he is at home. Somehow, we seldom get near enough to anything. The interest of all this coast which we had come to inspect was mainly literary and historical. And no country is of much interest until legends and poetry have draped it in hues that mere nature cannot produce. We looked at Nahant for Longfellow's sake; we strained our eyes to make out Marblehead on account of Whittier's ballad; we scrutinized the entrance to Salem Harbor because a genius once sat in its decaying custom-house and made of it a throne of the imagination. Upon this low shore line, which lies blinking in the midday sun, the waves of history have beaten for two centuries and a half, and romance has had time to grow there. Out of any of these coves might have sailed Sir Patrick Spens "to Noroway, to Noroway,"

"They hadna sailed upon the sea   A day but barely three,
Till loud and boisterous grew the wind,   And gurly grew the sea."

The sea was anything but gurly now; it lay idle and shining in an August holiday. It seemed as if we could sit all day and watch the suggestive shore and dream about it. But we could not. No man, and few women, can sit all day on those little round penitential stools that the company provide for the discomfort of their passengers. There is no scenery in the world that can be enjoyed from one of those stools. And when the traveler is at sea, with the land failing away in his horizon, and has to create his own scenery by an effort of the imagination, these stools are no assistance to him. The imagination, when one is sitting, will not work unless the back is supported. Besides, it began to be cold; notwithstanding the shiny, specious appearance of things, it was cold, except in a sheltered nook or two where the sun beat. This was nothing to be complained of by persons who had left the parching land in order to get cool. They knew that there would be a wind and a draught everywhere, and that they would be occupied nearly all the time in moving the little stools about to get out of the wind, or out of the sun, or out of something that is inherent in a steamboat. Most people enjoy riding on a steamboat, shaking and trembling and chow-chowing along in pleasant weather out of sight of land; and they do not feel any ennui, as may be inferred from the intense excitement which seizes them when a poor porpoise leaps from the water half a mile away. "Did you see the porpoise?" makes conversation for an hour. On our steamboat there was a man who said he saw a whale, saw him just as plain, off to the east, come up to blow; appeared to be a young one. I wonder where all these men come from who always see a whale. I never was on a sea-steamer yet that there was not one of these men.

We sailed from Boston Harbor straight for Cape Ann, and passed close by the twin lighthouses of Thacher, so near that we could see the lanterns and the stone gardens, and the young barbarians of Thacher all at play; and then we bore away, straight over the trackless Atlantic, across that part of the map where the title and the publisher's name are usually printed, for the foreign city of St. John. It was after we passed these lighthouses that we did n't see the whale, and began to regret the hard fate that took us away from a view of the Isles of Shoals. I am not tempted to introduce them into this sketch, much as its surface needs their romantic color, for truth is stronger in me than the love of giving a deceitful pleasure. There will be nothing in this record that we did not see, or might not have seen. For instance, it might not be wrong to describe a coast, a town, or an island that we passed while we were performing our morning toilets in our staterooms. The traveler owes a duty to his readers, and if he is now and then too weary or too indifferent to go out from the cabin to survey a prosperous village where a landing is made, he has no right to cause the reader to suffer by his indolence. He should describe the village.

I had intended to describe the Maine coast, which is as fascinating on the map as that of Norway. We had all the feelings appropriate to nearness to it, but we couldn't see it. Before we came abreast of it night had settled down, and there was around us only a gray and melancholy waste of salt water. To be sure it was a lovely night, with a young moon in its sky,

"I saw the new moon late yestreen
Wi' the auld moon in her arms,"

and we kept an anxious lookout for the Maine hills that push so boldly down
into the sea. At length we saw them,--faint, dusky shadows in the horizon, looming
up in an ashy color and with a most poetical light. We made out clearly Mt. Desert,
and felt repaid for our journey by the sight of this famous island, even at such a
distance. I pointed out the hills to the man at the wheel, and asked if we should go
any nearer to Mt. Desert.

"Them!" said he, with the merited contempt which officials in this country
have for inquisitive travelers,--"them's Camden Hills. You won't see Mt. Desert till
midnight, and then you won't."

One always likes to weave in a little romance with summer travel on a steamboat; and we came aboard this one with the purpose and the language to do so. But
there was an absolute want of material, that would hardly be credited if we went
into details. The first meeting of the passengers at the dinner-table revealed it. There
is a kind of female plainness which is pathetic, and many persons can truly say that
to them it is homelike; and there are vulgarities of manner that are interesting; and
there are peculiarities, pleasant or the reverse, which attract one's attention: but
there was absolutely nothing of this sort on our boat. The female passengers were
all neutrals, incapable, I should say, of making any impression whatever even under
the most favorable circumstances. They were probably women of the Provinces,
and took their neutral tint from the foggy land they inhabit, which is neither a republic nor a monarchy, but merely a languid expectation of something undefined.
My comrade was disposed to resent the dearth of beauty, not only on this vessel
but throughout the Provinces generally,--a resentment that could be shown to be
unjust, for this was evidently not the season for beauty in these lands, and it was
probably a bad year for it. Nor should an American of the United States be forward
to set up his standard of taste in such matters; neither in New Brunswick, Nova
Scotia, nor Cape Breton have I heard the inhabitants complain of the plainness of
the women.

On such a night two lovers might have been seen, but not on our boat, leaning
over the taffrail,--if that is the name of the fence around the cabin-deck, looking at

the moon in the western sky and the long track of light in the steamer's wake with unutterable tenderness. For the sea was perfectly smooth, so smooth as not to interfere with the most perfect tenderness of feeling; and the vessel forged ahead under the stars of the soft night with an adventurous freedom that almost concealed the commercial nature of her mission. It seemed --this voyaging through the sparkling water, under the scintillating heavens, this resolute pushing into the opening splendors of night --like a pleasure trip. "It is the witching hour of half past ten," said my comrade, "let us turn in." (The reader will notice the consideration for her feelings which has omitted the usual description of "a sunset at sea.")

When we looked from our state-room window in the morning we saw land. We were passing within a stone's throw of a pale-green and rather cold-looking coast, with few trees or other evidences of fertile soil. Upon going out I found that we were in the harbor of Eastport. I found also the usual tourist who had been up, shivering in his winter overcoat, since four o'clock. He described to me the magnificent sunrise, and the lifting of the fog from islands and capes, in language that made me rejoice that he had seen it. He knew all about the harbor. That wooden town at the foot of it, with the white spire, was Lubec; that wooden town we were approaching was Eastport. The long island stretching clear across the harbor was Campobello. We had been obliged to go round it, a dozen miles out of our way, to get in, because the tide was in such a stage that we could not enter by the Lubec Channel. We had been obliged to enter an American harbor by British waters.

We approached Eastport with a great deal of curiosity and considerable respect. It had been one of the cities of the imagination. Lying in the far east of our great territory, a military and even a sort of naval station, a conspicuous name on the map, prominent in boundary disputes and in war operations, frequent in telegraphic dispatches,--we had imagined it a solid city, with some Oriental, if decayed, peculiarity, a port of trade and commerce. The tourist informed me that Eastport looked very well at a distance, with the sun shining on its white houses. When we landed at its wooden dock we saw that it consisted of a few piles of lumber, a sprinkling of small cheap houses along a sidehill, a big hotel with a flag-staff, and a very peaceful looking arsenal. It is doubtless a very enterprising and deserving city, but its aspect that morning was that of cheapness, newness, and stagnation, with no compensating picturesqueness. White paint always looks chilly under a gray sky and on naked hills. Even in hot August the place seemed bleak. The tourist, who went ashore with a view to breakfast, said that it would be a good place to stay in and go a-fishing and picnicking on Campobello Island. It has another advantage for the wicked over other Maine towns. Owing to the contiguity of British territory, the Maine Law is constantly evaded, in spirit. The thirsty citizen or sailor has only to step into a boat and give it a shove or two across the narrow stream that separates the United States from Deer Island and land, when he can ruin his breath, and return before he is missed.

This might be a cause of war with, England, but it is not the most serious grievance here. The possession by the British of the island of Campobello is an insufferable menace and impertinence. I write with the full knowledge of what war is. We ought to instantly dislodge the British from Campobello. It entirely shuts up and commands our harbor, one of our chief Eastern harbors and war stations, where we keep a flag and cannon and some soldiers, and where the customs officers look out for smuggling. There is no way to get into our own harbor, except in favorable conditions of the tide, without begging the courtesy of a passage through British waters. Why is England permitted to stretch along down our coast in this straggling and inquisitive manner? She might almost as well own Long Island. It was impossible to prevent our cheeks mantling with shame as we thought of this, and saw ourselves, free American citizens, land-locked by alien soil in our own harbor.

We ought to have war, if war is necessary to possess Campobello and Deer Islands; or else we ought to give the British Eastport. I am not sure but the latter would be the better course.

With this war spirit in our hearts, we sailed away into the British waters of the Bay of Fundy, but keeping all the morning so close to the New Brunswick shore that we could see there was nothing on it; that is, nothing that would make one wish to land. And yet the best part of going to sea is keeping close to the shore, however tame it may be, if the weather is pleasant. A pretty bay now and then, a rocky cove with scant foliage, a lighthouse, a rude cabin, a level land, monotonous and without noble forests,--this was New Brunswick as we coasted along it under the most favorable circumstances. But we were advancing into the Bay of Fundy; and my comrade, who had been brought up on its high tides in the district school, was on the lookout for this phenomenon. The very name of Fundy is stimulating to the imagination, amid the geographical wastes of youth, and the young fancy reaches out to its tides with an enthusiasm that is given only to Fingal's Cave and other pictorial wonders of the text-book. I am sure the district schools would become what they are not now, if the geographers would make the other parts of the globe as attractive as the sonorous Bay of Fundy. The recitation about that is always an easy one; there is a lusty pleasure in the mere shouting out of the name, as if the speaking it were an innocent sort of swearing. From the Bay of Fundy the rivers run uphill half the time, and the tides are from forty to ninety feet high. For myself, I confess that, in my imagination, I used to see the tides of this bay go stalking into the land like gigantic waterspouts; or, when I was better instructed, I could see them advancing on the coast like a solid wall of masonry eighty feet high. "Where," we said, as we came easily, and neither uphill nor downhill, into the pleasant harbor of St. John,---"where are the tides of our youth?"

They were probably out, for when we came to the land we walked out upon the foot of a sloping platform that ran into the water by the side of the piles of the dock, which stood up naked and blackened high in the air. It is not the purpose of this paper to describe St. John, nor to dwell upon its picturesque situation. As one approaches it from the harbor it gives a promise which its rather shabby streets, decaying houses, and steep plank sidewalks do not keep. A city set on a hill, with flags flying from a roof here and there, and a few shining spires and walls glistening in the sun, always looks well at a distance. St. John is extravagant in the matter of flagstaffs; almost every well-to-do citizen seems to have one on his premises, as a sort of vent for his loyalty, I presume. It is a good fashion, at any rate, and its more general adoption by us would add to the gayety of our cities when we celebrate the birthday of the President. St. John is built on a steep sidehill, from which it would be in danger of sliding off, if its houses were not mortised into the solid rock. This makes the house-foundations secure, but the labor of blasting out streets is considerable. We note these things complacently as we toil in the sun up the hill to the Victoria Hotel, which stands well up on the backbone of the ridge, and from the upper windows of which we have a fine view of the harbor, and of the hill opposite, above Carleton, where there is the brokenly truncated ruin of a round stone tower. This tower was one of the first things that caught our eyes as we entered the harbor. It gave an antique picturesqueness to the landscape which it entirely wanted without this. Round stone towers are not so common in this world that we can afford to be indifferent to them. This is called a Martello tower, but I could not learn who built it. I could not understand the indifference, almost amounting to contempt, of the citizens of St. John in regard to this their only piece of curious antiquity. "It is nothing but the ruins of an old fort," they said; "you can see it as well from here as by going there." It was, however, the one thing at St. John I was determined to see. But we never got any nearer to it than the ferry-landing. Want of time and the vis inertia of the place were against us. And now, as I think of that tower and its perhaps mysterious origin, I have a longing for it that the possession of nothing else in the Provinces could satisfy.

But it must not be forgotten that we were on our way to Baddeck; that the whole purpose of the journey was to reach Baddeck; that St. John was only an incident in the trip; that any information about St. John, which is here thrown in or mercifully withheld, is entirely gratuitous, and is not taken into account in the price the reader pays for this volume. But if any one wants to know what sort of a place St. John is, we can tell him: it is the sort of a place that if you get into it after eight o'clock on Wednesday morning, you cannot get out of it in any direction until Thursday morning at eight o'clock, unless you want to smuggle goods on the night train to Bangor. It was eleven o'clock Wednesday forenoon when we arrived at St. John. The Intercolonial railway train had gone to Shediac; it had gone also on its roundabout Moncton, Missaquat River, Truro, Stewiack, and Shubenacadie way to Halifax; the boat had gone to Digby Gut and Annapolis to catch the train that way for Halifax; the boat had gone up the river to Frederick, the capital. We could go to none of these places till the next day. We had no desire to go to Frederick, but we made the fact that we were cut off from it an addition to our injury. The people of St. John have this peculiarity: they never start to go anywhere except early in the morning.

The reader to whom time is nothing does not yet appreciate the annoyance of our situation. Our time was strictly limited. The active world is so constituted that it could not spare us more than two weeks. We must reach Baddeck Saturday night or never. To go home without seeing Baddeck was simply intolerable. Had we not told everybody that we were going to Baddeck? Now, if we had gone to Shediac in the train that left St. John that morning, we should have taken the steamboat that would have carried us to Port Hawkesbury, whence a stage connected with a steamboat on the Bras d'Or, which (with all this profusion of relative pronouns) would land us at Baddeck on Friday. How many times had we been over this route on the map and the prospectus of travel! And now, what a delusion it seemed! There would not another boat leave Shediac on this route till the following Tuesday,--quite too late for our purpose. The reader sees where we were, and will be prepared, if he has a map (and any feelings), to appreciate the masterly strategy that followed.

II

During the pilgrimage everything does not suit the tastes of the pilgrim.

--TURKISH PROVERB.

One seeking Baddeck, as a possession, would not like to be detained a prisoner even in Eden,--much less in St. John, which is unlike Eden in several important respects. The tree of knowledge does not grow there, for one thing; at least St. John's ignorance of Baddeck amounts to a feature. This encountered us everywhere. So dense was this ignorance, that we, whose only knowledge of the desired place was obtained from the prospectus of travel, came to regard ourselves as missionaries of geographical information in this dark provincial city.

The clerk at the Victoria was not unwilling to help us on our journey, but if he could have had his way, we would have gone to a place on Prince Edward Island which used to be called Bedeque, but is now named Summerside, in the hope of attracting summer visitors. As to Cape Breton, he said the agent of the Intercolonial could tell us all about that, and put us on the route. We repaired to the agent. The kindness of this person dwells in our memory. He entered at once into our longings and perplexities. He produced his maps and time-tables, and showed us clearly what we already knew. The Port Hawkesbury steamboat from Shediac for that week had gone, to be sure, but we could take one of another line which would leave us at Pictou, whence we could take another across to Port Hood, on Cape Breton. This looked fair, until we showed the agent that there was no steamer to Port Hood.

"Ah, then you can go another way. You can take the Intercolonial railway round to Pictou, catch the steamer for Port Hawkesbury, connect with the steamer on the Bras d'Or, and you are all right."

So it would seem. It was a most obliging agent; and it took us half an hour to convince him that the train would reach Pictou half a day too late for the steamer, that no other boat would leave Pictou for Cape Breton that week, and that even if we could reach the Bras d'Or, we should have no means of crossing it, except by swimming. The perplexed agent thereupon referred us to Mr. Brown, a shipper on the wharf, who knew all about Cape Breton, and could tell us exactly how to get there. It is needless to say that a weight was taken off our minds. We pinned our faith to Brown, and sought him in his warehouse. Brown was a prompt business man, and a traveler, and would know every route and every conveyance from Nova Scotia to Cape Breton.

Mr. Brown was not in. He never is in. His store is a rusty warehouse, low and musty, piled full of boxes of soap and candles and dried fish, with a little glass cubby in one corner, where a thin clerk sits at a high desk, like a spider in his web. Perhaps he is a spider, for the cubby is swarming with flies, whose hum is the only noise of traffic; the glass of the window-sash has not been washed since it was put in apparently. The clerk is not writing, and has evidently no other use for his steel pen than spearing flies. Brown is out, says this young votary of commerce, and will not be in till half past five. We remark upon the fact that nobody ever is "in" these dingy warehouses, wonder when the business is done, and go out into the street to wait for Brown.

In front of the store is a dray, its horse fast-asleep, and waiting for the revival of commerce. The travelers note that the dray is of a peculiar construction, the body being dropped down from the axles so as nearly to touch the ground,--a great convenience in loading and unloading; they propose to introduce it into their native land. The dray is probably waiting for the tide to come in. In the deep slip lie a dozen helpless vessels, coasting schooners mostly, tipped on their beam ends in the mud, or propped up by side-pieces as if they were built for land as well as for water. At the end of the wharf is a long English steamboat unloading railroad iron, which will return to the Clyde full of Nova Scotia coal. We sit down on the dock, where the fresh sea-breeze comes up the harbor, watch the lazily swinging crane on the vessel, and meditate upon the greatness of England and the peacefulness of the drowsy after noon. One's feeling of rest is never complete--unless he can see somebody else at work, --but the labor must be without haste, as it is in the Provinces.

While waiting for Brown, we had leisure to explore the shops of King's Street, and to climb up to the grand triumphal arch which stands on top of the hill and guards the entrance to King's Square.

Of the shops for dry-goods I have nothing to say, for they tempt the unwary American to violate the revenue laws of his country; but he may safely go into the book-shops. The literature which is displayed in the windows and on the counters has lost that freshness which it once may have had, and is, in fact, if one must use the term, fly-specked, like the cakes in the grocery windows on the side streets. There are old illustrated newspapers from the States, cheap novels from the same, and the flashy covers of the London and Edinburgh sixpenny editions. But this is the dull season for literature, we reflect.

It will always be matter of regret to us that we climbed up to the triumphal arch, which appeared so noble in the distance, with the trees behind it. For when we reached it, we found that it was built of wood, painted and sanded, and in a shocking state of decay; and the grove to which it admitted us was only a scant assemblage of sickly locust-trees, which seemed to be tired of battling with the un-favorable climate, and had, in fact, already retired from the business of ornamental shade trees. Adjoining this square is an ancient cemetery, the surface of which has decayed in sympathy with the mouldering remains it covers, and is quite a model in this respect. I have called this cemetery ancient, but it may not be so, for its air of decay is thoroughly modern, and neglect, and not years, appears to have made it the melancholy place of repose it is. Whether it is the fashionable and favorite resort of the dead of the city we did not learn, but there were some old men sitting in its damp shades, and the nurses appeared to make it a rendezvous for their baby-carriages,--a cheerful place to bring up children in, and to familiarize their infant minds with the fleeting nature of provincial life. The park and burying-ground, it is scarcely necessary to say, added greatly to the feeling of repose which stole over us on this sunny day. And they made us long for Brown and his information about Baddeck.

But Mr. Brown, when found, did not know as much as the agent. He had been in Nova Scotia; he had never been in Cape Breton; but he presumed we would find no difficulty in reaching Baddeck by so and so, and so and so. We consumed valuable time in convincing Brown that his directions to us were impracticable and valueless, and then he referred us to Mr. Cope. An interview with Mr. Cope discouraged us; we found that we were imparting everywhere more geographical information than we were receiving, and as our own stock was small, we concluded that we should be unable to enlighten all the inhabitants of St. John upon the subject of Baddeck before we ran out. Returning to the hotel, and taking our destiny into our own hands, we resolved upon a bold stroke.

But to return for a moment to Brown. I feel that Brown has been let off too easily in the above paragraph. His conduct, to say the truth, was not such as we expected of a man in whom we had put our entire faith for half a day,--a long while to trust anybody in these times,--a man whom we had exalted as an encyclopedia of information, and idealized in every way. A man of wealth and liberal views and courtly manners we had decided Brown would be. Perhaps he had a suburban villa on the heights over-looking Kennebeckasis Bay, and, recognizing us as brothers in a common interest in Baddeck, not-withstanding our different nationality, would insist upon taking us to his house, to sip provincial tea with Mrs. Brown and Victoria Louise, his daughter. When, therefore, Mr. Brown whisked into his dingy office, and, but for our importunity, would have paid no more attention to us than to up-country customers without credit, and when he proved to be willingly, it seemed to us, ignorant of Baddeck, our feelings received a great shock. It is incomprehensible that a man in the position of Brown with so many boxes of soap and candles to dispose of--should be so ignorant of a neighboring province. We had heard of the cordial unity of the Provinces in the New Dominion. Heaven help it, if it depends upon such fellows as Brown! Of course, his directing us to Cope was a mere fetch. For as we have intimated, it would have taken us longer to have given Cope an idea of Baddeck, than it did to enlighten Brown. But we had no bitter feelings about Cope, for we never had reposed confidence in him.

Our plan of campaign was briefly this: To take the steamboat at eight o'clock, Thursday morning, for Digby Gut and Annapolis; thence to go by rail through the poetical Acadia down to Halifax; to turn north and east by rail from Halifax to New Glasgow, and from thence to push on by stage to the Gut of Canso. This would carry us over the entire length of Nova Scotia, and, with good luck, land us on Cape Breton Island Saturday morning. When we should set foot on that island, we trusted that we should be able to make our way to Baddeck, by walking, swimming, or riding, whichever sort of locomotion should be most popular in that province. Our imaginations were kindled by reading that the "most superb line of stages on the continent" ran from New Glasgow to the Gut of Canso. If the reader perfectly understands this programme, he has the advantage of the two travelers at the time they made it.

It was a gray morning when we embarked from St. John, and in fact a little drizzle of rain veiled the Martello tower, and checked, like the cross-strokes of a line engraving, the hill on which it stands. The miscellaneous shining of such a harbor appears best in a golden haze, or in the mist of a morning like this. We had expected days of fog in this region; but the fog seemed to have gone out with the high tides of the geography. And it is simple justice to these possessions of her Majesty, to say that in our two weeks' acquaintance of them they enjoyed as delicious weather as ever falls on sea and shore, with the exception of this day when we crossed the Bay of Fundy. And this day was only one of those cool interludes of low color, which an artist would be thankful to introduce among a group of brilliant pictures. Such a day rests the traveler, who is overstimulated by shifting scenes played upon by the dazzling sun. So the cool gray clouds spread a grateful umbrella above us as we ran across the Bay of Fundy, sighted the headlands of the Gut of Digby, and entered into the Annapolis Basin, and into the region of a romantic history. The white houses of Digby, scattered over the downs like a flock of washed sheep, had a somewhat chilly aspect, it is true, and made us long for the sun on them. But as I think of it now, I prefer to have the town and the pretty hillsides that stand about the basin in the light we saw them; and especially do I like to recall the high wooden pier at Digby, deserted by the tide and so blown by the wind that the passengers who came out on it, with their tossing drapery, brought to mind the windy Dutch harbors that Backhuysen painted. We landed a priest here, and it was a pleasure to see him as he walked along the high pier, his broad hat flapping, and the wind blowing his long skirts away from his ecclesiastical legs.

It was one of the coincidences of life, for which no one can account, that when we descended upon these coasts, the Governor-General of the Dominion was abroad in his Provinces. There was an air of expectation of him everywhere, and of preparation for his coming; his lordship was the subject of conversation on the Digby boat, his movements were chronicled in the newspapers, and the gracious bearing of the Governor and Lady Dufferin at the civic receptions, balls, and picnics was recorded with loyal satisfaction; even a literary flavor was given to the provincial journals by quotations from his lordship's condescension to letters in the "High Latitudes." It was not without pain, however, that even in this un-American region we discovered the old Adam of journalism in the disposition of the newspapers of St. John toward sarcasm touching the well-meant attempts to entertain the Governor and his lady in the provincial town of Halifax,--a disposition to turn, in short, upon the demonstrations of loyal worship the faint light of ridicule. There were those upon the boat who were journeying to Halifax to take part in the civic ball about to be given to their excellencies, and as we were going in the same direction, we shared in the feeling of satisfaction which proximity to the Great often excites.

We had other if not deeper causes of satisfaction. We were sailing along the gracefully moulded and tree-covered hills of the Annapolis Basin, and up the mildly picturesque river of that name, and we were about to enter what the provincials all enthusiastically call the Garden of Nova Scotia. This favored vale, skirted by low ranges of hills on either hand, and watered most of the way by the Annapolis River, extends from the mouth of the latter to the town of Windsor on the river Avon. We expected to see something like the fertile valleys of the Connecticut or the Mohawk. We should also pass through those meadows on the Basin of Minas which Mr. Longfellow has made more sadly poetical than any other spot on the Western Continent. It is,--this valley of the Annapolis,--in the belief of provincials, the most beautiful and blooming place in the world, with a soil and climate kind to the husbandman; a land of fair meadows, orchards, and vines. It was doubtless our own fault that this land did not look to us like a garden, as it does to the inhabitants of Nova Scotia; and it was not until we had traveled over the rest of the country, that we saw the appropriateness of the designation. The explanation is, that not so much is required of a garden here as in some other parts of the world. Excellent apples, none finer, are exported from this valley to England, and the quality of the potatoes is said to ap-proach an ideal perfection here. I should think that oats would ripen well also in a good year, and grass, for those who care for it, may be satisfactory. I should judge that the other products of this garden are fish and building-stone. But we anticipate. And have we forgotten the "murmuring pines and the hemlocks"?

Nobody, I suppose, ever travels here without believing that he sees these trees of the imagination, so forcibly has the poet projected them upon the uni-versal consciousness. But we were unable to see them, on this route.

It would be a brutal thing for us to take seats in the railway train at Annapolis, and leave the ancient town, with its modern houses and remains of old fortifications, without a thought of the romantic history which saturates the region. There is not much in the smart, new restaurant, where a tidy waiting-maid skillfully depreciates our currency in exchange for bread and cheese and ale, to recall the early drama of the French discovery and settlement. For it is to the French that we owe the poetical interest that still invests, like a garment, all these islands and bays, just as it is to the Spaniards that we owe the romance of the Florida coast. Every spot on this continent that either of these races has touched has a color that is wanting in the prosaic settlements of the English.

Without the historical light of French adventure upon this town and basin of Annapolis, or Port Royal, as they were first named, I confess that I should have no longing to stay here for a week; notwithstanding the guide-book distinctly says that this harbor has "a striking resemblance to the beautiful Bay of Naples." I am not offended at this remark, for it is the one always made about a harbor, and I am sure the passing traveler can stand it, if the Bay of Naples can. And yet this tranquil basin must have seemed a haven of peace to the first discoverers.

It was on a lovely summer day in 1604, that the Sieur de Monts and his comrades, Champlain and the Baron de Poutrincourt, beating about the shores of Nova Scotia, were invited by the rocky gateway of the Port Royal Basin. They entered the small inlet, says Mr. Parkman, when suddenly the narrow strait dilated into a broad and tranquil basin, compassed with sunny hills, wrapped with woodland verdure and alive with waterfalls. Poutrincourt was delighted with the scene, and would fain remove thither from France with his family. Since Poutrincourt's day, the hills have been somewhat denuded of trees, and the waterfalls are not now in sight; at least, not under such a gray sky as we saw.

The reader who once begins to look into the French occupancy of Acadia is in danger of getting into a sentimental vein, and sentiment is the one thing to be shunned in these days. Yet I cannot but stay, though the train should leave us, to pay my respectful homage to one of the most heroic of women, whose name recalls the most romantic incident in the history of this region. Out of this past there rises no figure so captivating to the imagination as that of Madame de la Tour. And it is noticeable that woman has a curious habit of coming to the front in critical moments of history, and performing some exploit that eclipses in brilliancy all the deeds of contemporary men; and the exploit usually ends in a pathetic tragedy, that fixes it forever in the sympathy of the world. I need not copy out of the pages of De Charlevoix the well-known story of Madame de la Tour; I only wish he had told us more about her. It is here at Port Royal that we first see her with her husband. Charles de St. Etienne, the Chevalier de la Tour,--there is a world of romance in these mere names,--was a Huguenot nobleman who had a grant of Port Royal and of La Hive, from Louis XIII. He ceded La Hive to Razilli, the governor-in-chief of the provinces, who took a fancy to it, for a residence. He was living peacefully at Port Royal in 1647, when the Chevalier d'Aunay Charnise, having succeeded his brother Razilli at La Hive, tired of that place and removed to Port Royal. De Charnise was a Catholic; the difference in religion might not have produced any unpleasantness, but the two noblemen could not agree in dividing the profits of the peltry trade,--each being covetous, if we may so express it, of the hide of the savage continent, and determined to take it off for himself. At any rate, disagreement arose, and De la Tour moved over to the St. John, of which region his father had enjoyed a grant from Charles I. of England,--whose sad fate it is not necessary now to recall to the reader's mind,--and built a fort at the mouth of the river. But the differences of the two ambitious Frenchmen could not be composed. De la Tour obtained aid from Governor Winthrop at Boston, thus verifying the Catholic prediction that the Huguenots would side with the enemies of France on occasion. De Charnise received orders from Louis to arrest De la Tour; but a little preliminary to the arrest was the possession of the fort of St. John, and this he could not obtain, although be sent all his force against it. Taking advantage, however, of the absence of De la Tour, who had a habit of roving about, he one day besieged St. John. Madame de la Tour headed the little handful of men in the fort, and made such a gallant resistance that De Charnise was obliged to draw off his fleet with the loss of thirty-three men,--a very serious loss, when the supply of men was as distant as France. But De Charnise would not be balked by a woman; he attacked again; and this time, one of the garrison, a Swiss, betrayed the fort, and let the invaders into the walls by an unguarded entrance. It was Easter morning when this misfortune occurred, but the peaceful influence of the day did not avail. When Madame saw that she was betrayed, her spirits did not quail; she took refuge with her little band in a detached part of the fort, and there made such a bold show of defense, that De Charnise was obliged to agree to the terms of her surrender, which she dictated. No sooner had this un-chivalrous fellow obtained possession of the fort and of this Historic Woman, than, overcome with a false shame that he had made terms with a woman, he violated his noble word, and condemned to death all the men, except one, who was spared on condition that he should be the executioner of the others. And the poltroon compelled the brave woman to witness the execution, with the added indignity of a rope round her neck,--or as De Charlevoix much more neatly expresses it, "obligea sa prisonniere d'assister a l'execution, la corde au cou."

To the shock of this horror the womanly spirit of Madame de la Tour suc-cumbed; she fell into a decline and died soon after. De la Tour, himself an exile from his province, wandered about the New World in his customary pursuit of peltry. He was seen at Quebec for two years. While there, he heard of the death of De Charnise, and straightway repaired to St. John. The widow of his late enemy re-ceived him graciously, and he entered into possession of the estate of the late occu-pant with the consent of all the heirs. To remove all roots of bitterness, De la Tour married Madame de Charnise, and history does not record any ill of either of them. I trust they had the grace to plant a sweetbrier on the grave of the noble woman to whose faithfulness and courage they owe their rescue from obscurity. At least the parties to this singular union must have agreed to ignore the lamented existence of the Chevalier d'Aunay.

With the Chevalier de la Tour, at any rate, it all went well thereafter. When Cromwell drove the French from Acadia, he granted great territorial rights to De la Tour, which that thrifty adventurer sold out to one of his co-grantees for L16,000; and he no doubt invested the money in peltry for the London market.

As we leave the station at Annapolis, we are obliged to put Madame de la Tour out of our minds to make room for another woman whose name, and we might say presence, fills all the valley before us. So it is that woman continues to reign, where she has once got a foothold, long after her dear frame has become dust. Evangeline, who is as real a personage as Queen Esther, must have been a different woman from

Madame de la Tour. If the latter had lived at Grand Pre, she would, I trust, have made it hot for the brutal English who drove the Acadians out of their salt-marsh paradise, and have died in her heroic shoes rather than float off into poetry. But if it should come to the question of marrying the De la Tour or the Evangeline, I think no man who was not engaged in the peltry trade would hesitate which to choose. At any rate, the women who love have more influence in the world than the women who fight, and so it happens that the sentimental traveler who passes through Port Royal without a tear for Madame de la Tour, begins to be in a glow of tender longing and regret for Evangeline as soon as he enters the valley of the Annapolis River. For myself, I expected to see written over the railway crossings the legend,

"Look out for Evangeline while the bell rings."

When one rides into a region of romance he does not much notice his speed or his carriage; but I am obliged to say that we were not hurried up the valley, and that the cars were not too luxurious for the plain people, priests, clergymen, and belles of the region, who rode in them. Evidently the latest fashions had not arrived in the Provinces, and we had an opportunity of studying anew those that had long passed away in the States, and of remarking how inappropriate a fashion is when it has ceased to be the fashion.

The river becomes small shortly after we leave Annapolis and before we reach Paradise. At this station of happy appellation we looked for the satirist who named it, but he has probably sold out and removed. If the effect of wit is produced by the sudden recognition of a remote resemblance, there was nothing witty in the naming of this station. Indeed, we looked in vain for the "garden" appearance of the valley. There was nothing generous in the small meadows or the thin orchards; and if large trees ever grew on the bordering hills, they have given place to rather stunted evergreens; the scraggy firs and balsams, in fact, possess Nova Scotia generally as we saw it,--and there is nothing more uninteresting and wearisome than large tracts of these woods. We are bound to believe that Nova Scotia has somewhere, or had, great pines and hemlocks that murmur, but we were not blessed with the sight of them. Slightly picturesque this valley is with its winding river and high hills guarding it, and perhaps a person would enjoy a foot-tramp down it; but, I think he would find little peculiar or interesting after he left the neighborhood of the Basin of Minas.

Before we reached Wolfville we came in sight of this basin and some of the estuaries and streams that run into it; that is, when the tide goes out; but they are only muddy ditches half the time. The Acadia College was pointed out to us at Wolfville by a person who said that it is a feeble institution, a remark we were sorry to hear of a place described as "one of the foremost seats of learning in the Province." But our regret was at once extinguished by the announcement that the next station was Grand Pre! We were within three miles of the most poetic place in North America.

There was on the train a young man from Boston, who said that he was born in Grand Pre. It seemed impossible that we should actually be near a person so felicitously born. He had a justifiable pride in the fact, as well as in the bride by his side, whom he was taking to see for the first time his old home. His local information, imparted to her, overflowed upon us; and when he found that we had read "Evangeline," his delight in making us acquainted with the scene of that poem was pleasant to see. The village of Grand Pre is a mile from the station; and perhaps the reader would like to know exactly what the traveler, hastening on to Baddeck, can see of the famous locality.

We looked over a well-grassed meadow, seamed here and there by beds of streams left bare by the receding tide, to a gentle swell in the ground upon which is a not heavy forest growth. The trees partly conceal the street of Grand Pre, which is only a road bordered by common houses. Beyond is the Basin of Minas, with its sedgy shore, its dreary flats; and beyond that projects a bold headland, standing perpendicular against the sky. This is the Cape Blomidon, and it gives a certain dignity to the picture.

The old Normandy picturesqueness has departed from the village of Grand Pre. Yankee settlers, we were told, possess it now, and there are no descendants of the French Acadians in this valley. I believe that Mr. Cozzens found some of them in humble circumstances in a village on the other coast, not far from Halifax, and it is there, probably, that the

"Maidens still wear their Norman caps and their kirtles of homespun, And by the evening fire repeat Evangeline's story, While from its rocky caverns the deep-voiced, neighboring ocean Speaks, and in accents disconsolate answers the wail of the forest."

At any rate, there is nothing here now except a faint tradition of the French Acadians; and the sentimental traveler who laments that they were driven out, and not left behind their dikes to rear their flocks, and cultivate the rural virtues, and live in the simplicity of ignorance, will temper his sadness by the reflection that it is to the expulsion he owes "Evangeline" and the luxury of his romantic grief. So that if the traveler is honest, and examines his own soul faithfully, he will not know what state of mind to cherish as he passes through this region of sorrow.

Our eyes lingered as long as possible and with all eagerness upon these meadows and marshes which the poet has made immortal, and we regretted that inexorable Baddeck would not permit us to be pilgrims for a day in this Acadian land. Just as I was losing sight of the skirt of trees at Grand Pre, a gentleman in the dress of a rural clergyman left his seat, and complimented me with this remark: "I perceive, sir, that you are fond of reading."

I could not but feel flattered by this unexpected discovery of my nature, which was no doubt due to the fact that I held in my hand one of the works of Charles Reade on social science, called "Love me Little, Love me Long," and I said, "Of some kinds, I am."

"Did you ever see a work called 'Evangeline'?"

"Oh, yes, I have frequently seen it."

"You may remember," continued this Mass of Information, "that there is an allusion in it to Grand Pre. That is the place, sir!"

"Oh, indeed, is that the place? Thank you."

"And that mountain yonder is Cape Blomidon, blow me down, you know."

And under cover of this pun, the amiable clergyman retired, unconscious, I presume, of his prosaic effect upon the atmosphere of the region. With this intrusion of the commonplace, I suffered an eclipse of faith as to Evangeline, and was not sorry to have my attention taken up by the river Avon, along the banks of which we were running about this time. It is really a broad arm of the basin, extending up to Windsor, and beyond in a small stream, and would have been a charming river if there had been a drop of water in it. I never knew before how much water adds to a river. Its slimy bottom was quite a ghastly spectacle, an ugly gash in the land that nothing could heal but the friendly returning tide. I should think it would be confusing to dwell by a river that runs first one way and then the other, and then vanishes altogether.

All the streams about this basin are famous for their salmon and shad, and the season for these fish was not yet passed. There seems to be an untraced affinity between the shad and the strawberry; they appear and disappear in a region simultaneously. When we reached Cape Breton, we were a day or two late for both. It is impossible not to feel a little contempt for people who do not have these luxuries till July and August; but I suppose we are in turn despised by the Southerners because we do not have them till May and June. So, a great part of the enjoyment of life is in the knowledge that there are people living in a worse place than that you inhabit.

Windsor, a most respectable old town round which the railroad sweeps, with its iron bridge, conspicuous King's College, and handsome church spire, is a great place for plaster and limestone, and would be a good location for a person interested in these substances. Indeed, if a man can live on rocks, like a goat, he may settle anywhere between Windsor and Halifax. It is one of the most sterile regions in the Province. With the exception of a wild pond or two, we saw nothing but rocks and stunted firs, for forty-five miles, a monotony unrelieved by one picturesque feature. Then we longed for the "Garden of Nova Scotia," and understood what is meant by the name.

A member of the Ottawa government, who was on his way to the Governor-General's ball at Halifax, informed us that this country is rich in minerals, in iron especially, and he pointed out spots where gold had been washed out. But we do not covet it. And we were not sorry to learn from this gentleman, that since the formation of the Dominion, there is less and less desire in the Provinces for annexation to the United States. One of the chief pleasures in traveling in Nova Scotia now is in the constant reflection that you are in a foreign country; and annexation would take that away.

It is nearly dark when we reach the head of the Bedford Basin. The noble harbor of Halifax narrows to a deep inlet for three miles along the rocky slope on which the city stands, and then suddenly expands into this beautiful sheet of water. We ran along its bank for five miles, cheered occasionally by a twinkling light on the shore, and then came to a stop at the shabby terminus, three miles out of town. This basin is almost large enough to float the navy of Great Britain, and it could lie here, with the narrows fortified, secure from the attacks of the American navy, hovering outside in the fog. With these patriotic thoughts we enter the town. It is not the fault of the railroad, but its present inability to climb a rocky hill, that it does not run into the city. The suburbs are not impressive in the night, but they look better then than they do in the daytime; and the same might be said of the city itself. Probably there is not anywhere a more rusty, forlorn town, and this in spite of its magnificent situation.

It is a gala-night when we rattle down the rough streets, and have pointed out to us the somber government buildings. The Halifax Club House is a blaze of light, for the Governor-General is being received there, and workmen are still busy decorating the Provincial Building for the great ball. The city is indeed pervaded by his lordship, and we regret that we cannot see it in its normal condition of quiet; the hotels are full, and it is impossible to escape the festive feeling that is abroad. It ill accords with our desires, as tranquil travelers, to be plunged into such a vortex of slow dissipation. These people take their pleasures more gravely than we do, and probably will last the longer for their moderation. Having ascertained that we can get no more information about Baddeck here than in St. John, we go to bed early, for we are to depart from this fascinating place at six o'clock.

If any one objects that we are not competent to pass judgment on the city of Halifax by sleeping there one night, I beg leave to plead the usual custom of travelers,--where would be our books of travel, if more was expected than a night in a place?--and to state a few facts. The first is, that I saw the whole of Halifax. If I were inclined, I could describe it building by building. Cannot one see it all from the citadel hill, and by walking down by the horticultural garden and the Roman Catholic cemetery? and did not I climb that hill through the most dilapidated rows of brown houses, and stand on the greensward of the fortress at five o'clock in the morning, and see the whole city, and the British navy riding at anchor, and the fog coming in from the Atlantic Ocean? Let the reader go to! and if he would know more of Halifax, go there. We felt that if we remained there through the day, it would be a day of idleness and sadness. I could draw a picture of Halifax. I could relate its century of history; I could write about its free-school system, and its many noble charities. But the reader always skips such things. He hates information; and he himself would not stay in this dull garrison town any longer than he was obliged to.

There was to be a military display that day in honor of the Governor.

"Why," I asked the bright and light-minded colored boy who sold papers on the morning train, "don't you stay in the city and see it?"

"Pho," said he, with contempt, "I'm sick of 'em. Halifax is played out, and I'm going to quit it."

The withdrawal of this lively trader will be a blow to the enterprise of the place.

When I returned to the hotel for breakfast--which was exactly like the supper, and consisted mainly of green tea and dry toast--there was a commotion among the waiters and the hack-drivers over a nervous little old man, who was in haste to depart for the morning train. He was a specimen of provincial antiquity such as could not be seen elsewhere. His costume was of the oddest: a long-waisted coat reaching nearly to his heels, short trousers, a flowered silk vest, and a napless hat. He carried his baggage tied up in mealbags, and his attention was divided between that and two buxom daughters, who were evidently enjoying their first taste of city life. The little old man, who was not unlike a petrified Frenchman of the last century, had risen before daylight, roused up his daughters, and had them down on the sidewalk by four o'clock, waiting for hack, or horse-car, or something to take them to the station. That he might be a man of some importance at home was evident, but he had lost his head in the bustle of this great town, and was at the mercy of all advisers, none of whom could understand his mongrel language. As we came out to take the horse-car, he saw his helpless daughters driven off in one hack, while he was raving among his meal-bags on the sidewalk. Afterwards we saw him at the station, flying about in the greatest excitement, asking everybody about the train; and at last he found his way into the private office of the ticket-seller. "Get out of here!" roared that official. The old man persisted that he wanted a ticket. "Go round to the window; clear out!" In a very flustered state he was hustled out of the room. When he came to the window and made known his destination, he was refused tickets, because his train did not start for two hours yet!

This mercurial old gentleman only appears in these records because he was the only person we saw in this Province who was in a hurry to do anything, or to go anywhere.

We cannot leave Halifax without remarking that it is a city of great private virtue, and that its banks are sound. The appearance of its paper-money is not, however, inviting. We of the United States lead the world in beautiful paper-money; and when I exchanged my crisp, handsome greenbacks for the dirty, flimsy, ill-executed notes of the Dominion, at a dead loss of value, I could not be reconciled to the transaction. I sarcastically called the stuff I received "Confederate money;" but probably no one was wounded by the severity; for perhaps no one knew what a resemblance in badness there is between the "Confederate" notes of our civil war and the notes of the Dominion; and, besides, the Confederacy was too popular in the Provinces for the name to be a reproach to them. I wish I had thought of something more insulting to say.

By noon on Friday we came to New Glasgow, having passed through a country where wealth is to be won by hard digging if it is won at all; through Truro, at the head of the Cobequid Bay, a place exhibiting more thrift than any we have seen. A pleasant enough country, on the whole, is this which the road runs through up the Salmon and down the East River. New Glasgow is not many miles from Pictou, on the great Cumberland Strait; the inhabitants build vessels, and strangers drive out from here to see the neighboring coal mines. Here we were to dine and take the stage for a ride of eighty miles to the Gut of Canso.

The hotel at New Glasgow we can commend as one of the most unwholesome in the Province; but it is unnecessary to emphasize its condition, for if the traveler is in search of dirty hotels, he will scarcely go amiss anywhere in these regions. There seems to be a fashion in diet which endures. The early travelers as well as the later in these Atlantic provinces all note the prevalence of dry, limp toast and green tea; they are the staples of all the meals; though authorities differ in regard to the third element for discouraging hunger: it is sometimes boiled salt-fish and sometimes it is ham. Toast was probably an inspiration of the first woman of this part of the New World, who served it hot; but it has become now a tradition blindly followed, without regard to temperature; and the custom speaks volumes for the non-inventiveness of woman. At the inn in New Glasgow those who choose dine in their shirt-sleeves, and those skilled in the ways of this table get all they want in seven minutes. A man who understands the use of edged tools can get along twice as fast with a knife and fork as he can with a fork alone.

But the stage is at the door; the coach and four horses answer the advertisement of being "second to none on the continent." We mount to the seat with the driver. The sun is bright; the wind is in the southwest; the leaders are impatient to go; the start for the long ride is propitious.

But on the back seat in the coach is the inevitable woman, young and sickly, with the baby in her arms. The woman has paid her fare through to Guysborough, and holds her ticket. It turns out, however, that she wants to go to the district of Guysborough, to St. Mary's Cross Roads, somewhere in it, and not to the village of Guysborough, which is away down on Chedabucto Bay. (The reader will notice this geographical familiarity.) And this stage does not go in the direction of St. Mary's. She will not get out, she will not surrender her ticket, nor pay her fare again. Why should she? And the stage proprietor, the stage-driver, and the hostler mull over the problem, and sit down on the woman's hair trunk in front of the tavern to reason with her. The baby joins its voice from the coach window in the clamor of the discussion. The baby prevails. The stage company comes to a compromise, the woman dismounts, and we are off, away from the white houses, over the sandy road, out upon a hilly and not cheerful country. And the driver begins to tell us stories of winter hardships, drifted highways, a land buried in snow, and great peril to men and cattle.

III

"It was then summer, and the weather very fine; so pleased was I with the country, in which I had never travelled before, that my delight proved equal to my wonder."

--BENVENUTO CELLINI.

There are few pleasures in life equal to that of riding on the box-seat of a stage-coach, through a country unknown to you and hearing the driver talk about his horses. We made the intimate acquaintance of twelve horses on that day's ride, and learned the peculiar disposition and traits of each one of them, their ambition of display, their sensitiveness to praise or blame, their faithfulness, their playfulness, the readiness with which they yielded to kind treatment, their daintiness about food and lodging.

May I never forget the spirited little jade, the off-leader in the third stage, the petted belle of the route, the nervous, coquettish, mincing mare of Marshy Hope. A spoiled beauty she was; you could see that as she took the road with dancing step, tossing her pretty head about, and conscious of her shining black coat and her tail done up "in any simple knot,"--like the back hair of Shelley's Beatrice Cenci. How she ambled and sidled and plumed herself, and now and then let fly her little heels high in air in mere excess of larkish feeling.

"So! girl; so! Kitty," murmurs the driver in the softest tones of admiration; "she don't mean anything by it, she's just like a kitten."

But the heels keep flying above the traces, and by and by the driver is obliged to "speak hash" to the beauty. The reproof of the displeased tone is evidently felt, for she settles at once to her work, showing perhaps a little impatience, jerking her head up and down, and protesting by her nimble movements against the more deliberate trot of her companion. I believe that a blow from the cruel lash would have broken her heart; or else it would have made a little fiend of the spirited creature. The lash is hardly ever good for the sex.

For thirteen years, winter and summer, this coachman had driven this monotonous, uninteresting route, with always the same sandy hills, scrubby firs, occasional cabins, in sight. What a time to nurse his thought and feed on his heart! How deliberately he can turn things over in his brain! What a system of philosophy he might evolve out of his consciousness! One would think so. But, in fact, the stagebox is no place for thinking. To handle twelve horses every day, to keep each to its proper work, stimulating the lazy and restraining the free, humoring each disposition, so that the greatest amount of work shall be obtained with the least friction, making each trip on time, and so as to leave each horse in as good condition at the close as at the start, taking advantage of the road, refreshing the team by an occasional spurt of speed,--all these things require constant attention; and if the driver was composing an epic, the coach might go into the ditch, or, if no accident happened, the horses would be worn out in a month, except for the driver's care.

I conclude that the most delicate and important occupation in life is stage-driving. It would be easier to "run" the Treasury Department of the United States than a four-in-hand. I have a sense of the unimportance of everything else in comparison with this business in hand. And I think the driver shares that feeling. He is the autocrat of the situation. He is lord of all the humble passengers, and they feel their inferiority. They may have knowledge and skill in some things, but they are of no use here. At all the stables the driver is king; all the people on the route are deferential to him; they are happy if he will crack a joke with them, and take it as a favor if he gives them better than they send. And it is his joke that always raises the laugh, regardless of its quality.

We carry the royal mail, and as we go along drop little sealed canvas bags at way offices. The bags would not hold more than three pints of meal, and I can see that there is nothing in them. Yet somebody along here must be expecting a letter, or they would not keep up the mail facilities. At French River we change horses. There is a mill here, and there are half a dozen houses, and a cranky bridge, which the driver thinks will not tumble down this trip. The settlement may have seen better days, and will probably see worse.

I preferred to cross the long, shaky wooden bridge on foot, leaving the inside passengers to take the risk, and get the worth of their money; and while the horses were being put to, I walked on over the hill. And here I encountered a veritable foot-pad, with a club in his hand and a bundle on his shoulder, coming down the dusty road, with the wild-eyed aspect of one who travels into a far country in search of adventure. He seemed to be of a cheerful and sociable turn, and desired that I should linger and converse with him. But he was more meagerly supplied with the media of conversation than any person I ever met. His opening address was in a tongue that failed to convey to me the least idea. I replied in such language as I had with me, but it seemed to be equally lost upon him. We then fell back upon gestures and ejaculations, and by these I learned that he was a native of Cape Breton, but not an aborigine. By signs he asked me where I came from, and where I was going; and he was so much pleased with my destination, that he desired to know my name; and this I told him with all the injunction of secrecy I could convey; but he could no more pronounce it than I could speak his name. It occurred to me that perhaps he spoke a French patois, and I asked him; but he only shook his head. He would own neither to German nor Irish. The happy thought came to me of inquiring if he knew English. But he shook his head again, and said,

"No English, plenty garlic."

This was entirely incomprehensible, for I knew that garlic is not a language, but a smell. But when he had repeated the word several times, I found that he meant Gaelic; and when we had come to this understanding, we cordially shook hands and willingly parted. One seldom encounters a wilder or more good-natured savage than this stalwart wanderer. And meeting him raised my hopes of Cape Breton.

We change horses again, for the last stage, at Marshy Hope. As we turn down the hill into this place of the mournful name, we dash past a procession of five country wagons, which makes way for us: everything makes way for us; even death itself turns out for the stage with four horses. The second wagon carries a long box, which reveals to us the mournful errand of the caravan. We drive into the stable, and get down while the fresh horses are put to. The company's stables are all alike, and open at each end with great doors. The stable is the best house in the place; there are three or four houses besides, and one of them is white, and has vines growing over the front door, and hollyhocks by the front gate. Three or four women, and as many barelegged girls, have come out to look at the procession, and we lounge towards the group.

"It had a winder in the top of it, and silver handles," says one.

"Well, I declare; and you could 'a looked right in?"

"If I'd been a mind to."

"Who has died?" I ask.

"It's old woman Larue; she lived on Gilead Hill, mostly alone. It's better for her."

"Had she any friends?"

"One darter. They're takin' her over Eden way, to bury her where she come from."

"Was she a good woman?" The traveler is naturally curious to know what sort of people die in Nova Scotia.

"Well, good enough. Both her husbands is dead."

The gossips continued talking of the burying. Poor old woman Larue! It was mournful enough to encounter you for the only time in this world in this plight, and to have this glimpse of your wretched life on lonesome Gilead Hill. What pleasure, I wonder, had she in her life, and what pleasure have any of these hard-favored women in this doleful region? It is pitiful to think of it. Doubtless, however, the region isn't doleful, and the sentimental traveler would not have felt it so if he had not encountered this funereal flitting.

But the horses are in. We mount to our places; the big doors swing open.

"Stand away," cries the driver.

The hostler lets go Kitty's bridle, the horses plunge forward, and we are off at a gallop, taking the opposite direction from that pursued by old woman Larue.

This last stage is eleven miles, through a pleasanter country, and we make it in a trifle over an hour, going at an exhilarating gait, that raises our spirits out of the Marshy Hope level. The perfection of travel is ten miles an hour, on top of a stagecoach; it is greater speed than forty by rail. It nurses one's pride to sit aloft, and rattle past the farmhouses, and give our dust to the cringing foot tramps. There is something royal in the swaying of the coach body, and an excitement in the patter of the horses' hoofs. And what an honor it must be to guide such a machine through a region of rustic admiration!

The sun has set when we come thundering down into the pretty Catholic village of Antigonish,--the most home-like place we have seen on the island. The twin stone towers of the unfinished cathedral loom up large in the fading light, and the bishop's palace on the hill--the home of the Bishop of Arichat--appears to be an imposing white barn with many staring windows. At Antigonish--with the emphasis on the last syllable--let the reader know there is a most comfortable inn, kept by a cheery landlady, where the stranger is served by the comely handmaidens, her daughters, and feels that he has reached a home at last. Here we wished to stay. Here we wished to end this weary pilgrimage. Could Baddeck be as attractive as this peaceful valley? Should we find any inn on Cape Breton like this one?

"Never was on Cape Breton," our driver had said; "hope I never shall be. Heard enough about it. Taverns? You'll find 'em occupied."

"Fleas?

"Wus."

"But it is a lovely country?"

"I don't think it."

Into what unknown dangers were we going? Why not stay here and be happy? It was a soft summer night. People were loitering in the street; the young beaux of the place going up and down with the belles, after the leisurely manner in youth and summer; perhaps they were students from St. Xavier College, or visiting gallants from Guysborough. They look into the post-office and the fancy store. They stroll and take their little provincial pleasure and make love, for all we can see, as if Antigonish were a part of the world. How they must look down on Marshy Hope and Addington Forks and Tracadie! What a charming place to live in is this!

But the stage goes on at eight o'clock. It will wait for no man. There is no other stage till eight the next night, and we have no alternative but a night ride. We put aside all else except duty and Baddeck. This is strictly a pleasure-trip.

The stage establishment for the rest of the journey could hardly be called the finest on the continent. The wagon was drawn by two horses. It was a square box, covered with painted cloth. Within were two narrow seats, facing each other, affording no room for the legs of passengers, and offering them no position but a strictly upright one. It was a most ingeniously uncomfortable box in which to put sleepy travelers for the night. The weather would be chilly before morning, and to sit upright on a narrow board all night, and shiver, is not cheerful. Of course, the reader says that this is no hardship to talk about. But the reader is mistaken. Anything is a hardship when it is unpleasantly what one does not desire or expect. These travelers had spent wakeful nights, in the forests, in a cold rain, and never thought of complaining. It is useless to talk about the Polar sufferings of Dr. Kane to a guest at a metropolitan hotel, in the midst of luxury, when the mosquito sings all night in his ear, and his mutton-chop is overdone at breakfast. One does not like to be set up for a hero in trifles, in odd moments, and in inconspicuous places.

There were two passengers besides ourselves, inhabitants of Cape Breton Island, who were returning from Halifax to Plaster Cove, where they were engaged in the occupation of distributing alcoholic liquors at retail. This fact we ascertained incidentally, as we learned the nationality of our comrades by their brogue, and their religion by their lively ejaculations during the night. We stowed ourselves into the rigid box, bade a sorrowing good-night to the landlady and her daughters, who stood at the inn door, and went jingling down the street towards the open country.

The moon rises at eight o'clock in Nova Scotia. It came above the horizon exactly as we began our journey, a harvest-moon, round and red. When I first saw it, it lay on the edge of the horizon as if too heavy to lift itself, as big as a cart-wheel, and its disk cut by a fence-rail. With what a flood of splendor it deluged farmhouses and farms, and the broad sweep of level country! There could not be a more magnificent night in which to ride towards that geographical mystery of our boyhood, the Gut of Canso.

A few miles out of town the stage stopped in the road before a post-station. An old woman opened the door of the farmhouse to receive the bag which the driver carried to her. A couple of sprightly little girls rushed out to "interview" the passengers, climbing up to ask their names and, with much giggling, to get a peep at their faces. And upon the handsomeness or ugliness of the faces they saw in the moonlight they pronounced with perfect candor. We are not obliged to say what their verdict was. Girls here, no doubt, as elsewhere, lose this trustful candor as they grow older.

Just as we were starting, the old woman screamed out from the door, in a shrill voice, addressing the driver, "Did you see ary a sick man 'bout 'Tigonish?"

"Nary."

"There's one been round here for three or four days, pretty bad off; 's got the St. Vitus's. He wanted me to get him some medicine for it up to Antigonish. I've got it here in a vial, and I wished you could take it to him."

"Where is he?"

"I dunno. I heern he'd gone east by the Gut. Perhaps you'll hear of him." All this screamed out into the night.

"Well, I'll take it."

We took the vial aboard and went on; but the incident powerfully affected us. The weird voice of the old woman was exciting in itself, and we could not escape the image of this unknown man, dancing about this region without any medicine, fleeing perchance by night and alone, and finally flitting away down the Gut of Canso. This fugitive mystery almost immediately shaped itself into the following simple poem:

"There was an old man of Canso, Unable to sit or stan' so. When I asked him why he ran so, Says he, 'I've St. Vitus' dance so, All down the Gut of Canso.'"

This melancholy song is now, I doubt not, sung by the maidens of Antigonish.

In spite of the consolations of poetry, however, the night wore on slowly, and soothing sleep tried in vain to get a lodgment in the jolting wagon. One can sleep upright, but not when his head is every moment knocked against the framework of a wagon-cover. Even a jolly young Irishman of Plaster Cove, whose nature it is to sleep under whatever discouragement, is beaten by these circumstances. He wishes he had his fiddle along. We never know what men are on casual acquaintance. This rather stupid-looking fellow is a devotee of music, and knows how to coax the sweetness out of the unwilling violin. Sometimes he goes miles and miles on winter nights to draw the seductive bow for the Cape Breton dancers, and there is enthusiasm in his voice, as he relates exploits of fiddling from sunset till the dawn of day. Other information, however, the young man has not; and when this is exhausted, he becomes sleepy again, and tries a dozen ways to twist himself into a posture in which sleep will be possible. He doubles up his legs, he slides them under the seat, he sits on the wagon bottom; but the wagon swings and jolts and knocks him about. His patience under this punishment is admirable, and there is something pathetic in his restraint from profanity.

It is enough to look out upon the magnificent night; the moon is now high, and swinging clear and distant; the air has grown chilly; the stars cannot be eclipsed by the greater light, but glow with a chastened fervor. It is on the whole a splendid display for the sake of four sleepy men, banging along in a coach,--an insignificant little vehicle with two horses. No one is up at any of the farmhouses to see it; no one appears to take any interest in it, except an occasional baying dog, or a rooster that has mistaken the time of night. By midnight we come to Tracadie, an orchard, a farmhouse, and a stable. We are not far from the sea now, and can see a silver mist in the north. An inlet comes lapping up by the old house with a salty smell and a suggestion of oyster-beds. We knock up the sleeping hostlers, change horses, and go on again, dead sleepy, but unable to get a wink. And all the night is blazing with beauty. We think of the criminal who was sentenced to be kept awake till he died.

The fiddler makes another trial. Temperately remarking, "I am very sleepy," he kneels upon the floor and rests his head on the seat. This position for a second promises repose; but almost immediately his head begins to pound the seat, and beat a lively rat-a-plan on the board. The head of a wooden idol couldn't stand this treatment more than a minute. The fiddler twisted and turned, but his head went like a triphammer on the seat. I have never seen a devotional attitude so deceptive, or one that produced less favorable results. The young man rose from his knees, and meekly said,

"It's dam hard."

If the recording angel took down this observation, he doubtless made a note of the injured tone in which it was uttered.

How slowly the night passes to one tipping and swinging along in a slowly moving stage! But the harbinger of the day came at last. When the fiddler rose from his knees, I saw the morning-star burst out of the east like a great diamond, and I knew that Venus was strong enough to pull up even the sun, from whom she is never distant more than an eighth of the heavenly circle. The moon could not put her out of countenance. She blazed and scintillated with a dazzling brilliance, a throbbing splendor, that made the moon seem a pale, sentimental invention. Steadily she mounted, in her fresh beauty, with the confidence and vigor of new love, driving her more domestic rival out of the sky. And this sort of thing, I suppose, goes on frequently. These splendors burn and this panorama passes night after night down at the end of Nova Scotia, and all for the stage-driver, dozing along on his box, from Antigonish to the strait.

"Here you are," cries the driver, at length, when we have become wearily indifferent to where we are. We have reached the ferry. The dawn has not come, but it is not far off. We step out and find a chilly morning, and the dark waters of the Gut of Canso flowing before us lighted here and there by a patch of white mist. The ferryman is asleep, and his door is shut. We call him by all the names known among men. We pound upon his house, but he makes no sign. Before he awakes and comes out, growling, the sky in the east is lightened a shade, and the star of the dawn sparkles less brilliantly. But the process is slow. The twilight is long. There is a surprising deliberation about the preparation of the sun for rising, as there is in the movements of the boatman. Both appear to be reluctant to begin the day.

The ferryman and his shaggy comrade get ready at last, and we step into the clumsy yawl, and the slowly moving oars begin to pull us upstream. The strait is here less than a mile wide; the tide is running strongly, and the water is full of swirls,--the little whirlpools of the rip-tide. The morning-star is now high in the sky; the moon, declining in the west, is more than ever like a silver shield; along the east is a faint flush of pink. In the increasing light we can see the bold shores of the strait, and the square projection of Cape Porcupine below.

On the rocks above the town of Plaster Cove, where there is a black and white sign,--Telegraph Cable,--we set ashore our companions of the night, and see them climb up to their station for retailing the necessary means of intoxication in their district, with the mournful thought that we may never behold them again.

As we drop down along the shore, there is a white sea-gull asleep on the rock, rolled up in a ball, with his head under his wing. The rock is dripping with dew, and the bird is as wet as his hard bed. We pass within an oar's length of him, but he does not heed us, and we do not disturb his morning slumbers. For there is no such cruelty as the waking of anybody out of a morning nap.

When we land, and take up our bags to ascend the hill to the white tavern of Port Hastings (as Plaster Cove now likes to be called), the sun lifts himself slowly over the treetops, and the magic of the night vanishes.

And this is Cape Breton, reached after almost a week of travel. Here is the Gut of Canso, but where is Baddeck? It is Saturday morning; if we cannot make Baddeck by night, we might as well have remained in Boston. And who knows what we shall find if we get there? A forlorn fishing-station, a dreary hotel? Suppose we cannot get on, and are forced to stay here? Asking ourselves these questions, we enter the Plaster Cove tavern. No one is stirring, but the house is open, and we take possession of the dirty public room, and almost immediately drop to sleep in the fluffy rocking-chairs; but even sleep is not strong enough to conquer our desire to push on, and we soon rouse up and go in pursuit of information.

No landlord is to be found, but there is an unkempt servant in the kitchen, who probably does not see any use in making her toilet more than once a week. To this fearful creature is intrusted the dainty duty of preparing breakfast. Her indifference is equal to her lack of information, and her ability to convey information is fettered by her use of Gaelic as her native speech. But she directs us to the stable. There we find a driver hitching his horses to a two-horse stage-wagon.

"Is this stage for Baddeck?"

"Not much."

"Is there any stage for Baddeck?"

"Not to-day."

"Where does this go, and when?"

"St. Peter's. Starts in fifteen minutes."

This seems like "business," and we are inclined to try it, especially as we have no notion where St. Peter's is.

"Does any other stage go from here to-day anywhere else?"

"Yes. Port Hood. Quarter of an hour."

Everything was about to happen in fifteen minutes. We inquire further. St. Peter's is on the east coast, on the road to Sydney. Port Hood is on the west coast. There is a stage from Port Hood to Baddeck. It would land us there some time Sunday morning; distance, eighty miles.

Heavens! what a pleasure-trip. To ride eighty miles more without sleep! We should simply be delivered dead on the Bras d'Or; that is all. Tell us, gentle driver, is there no other way?

"Well, there's Jim Hughes, come over at midnight with a passenger from Baddeck; he's in the hotel now; perhaps he'll take you."

Our hope hung on Jim Hughes. The frowzy servant piloted us up to his sleeping-room. "Go right in," said she; and we went in, according to the simple custom of the country, though it was a bedroom that one would not enter except on business. Mr. Hughes did not like to be disturbed, but he proved himself to be a man who could wake up suddenly, shake his head, and transact business,--a sort of Napoleon, in fact. Mr. Hughes stared at the intruders for a moment, as if he meditated an assault.

"Do you live in Baddeck?" we asked.

"No; Hogamah,--half-way there."

"Will you take us to Baddeck to-day?"

Mr. Hughes thought. He had intended to sleep--till noon. He had then intended to go over the Judique Mountain and get a boy. But he was disposed to accommodate. Yes, for money--sum named--he would give up his plans, and start for Baddeck in an hour. Distance, sixty miles. Here was a man worth having; he could come to a decision before he was out of bed. The bargain was closed.

We would have closed any bargain to escape a Sunday in the Plaster Cove hotel. There are different sorts of hotel uncleanliness. There is the musty old inn, where the dirt has accumulated for years, and slow neglect has wrought a picturesque sort of dilapidation, the mouldiness of time, which has something to recommend it. But there is nothing attractive in new nastiness, in the vulgar union of smartness and filth. A dirty modern house, just built, a house smelling of poor whiskey and vile tobacco, its white paint grimy, its floors unclean, is ever so much worse than an old inn that never pretended to be anything but a rookery. I say nothing against the hotel at Plaster Cove. In fact, I recommend it. There is a kind of harmony about it that I like. There is a harmony between the breakfast and the frowzy Gaelic cook we saw "sozzling" about in the kitchen. There is a harmony between the appearance of the house and the appearance of the buxom young housekeeper who comes upon the scene later, her hair saturated with the fatty matter of the bear. The traveler will experience a pleasure in paying his bill and departing.

Although Plaster Cove seems remote on the map, we found that we were right in the track of the world's news there. It is the transfer station of the Atlantic Cable Company, where it exchanges messages with the Western Union. In a long wooden building, divided into two main apartments, twenty to thirty operators are employed. At eight o'clock the English force was at work receiving the noon messages from London. The American operators had not yet come on, for New York business would not begin for an hour. Into these rooms is poured daily the news of the world, and these young fellows toss it about as lightly as if it were household gossip. It is a marvelous exchange, however, and we had intended to make some reflections here upon the en rapport feeling, so to speak, with all the world, which we experienced while there; but our conveyance was waiting. We telegraphed our coming to Baddeck, and departed. For twenty-five cents one can send a dispatch to any part of the Dominion, except the region where the Western Union has still a foothold.

Our conveyance was a one-horse wagon, with one seat. The horse was well enough, but the seat was narrow for three people, and the entire establishment had in it not much prophecy of Baddeck for that day. But we knew little of the power of Cape Breton driving. It became evident that we should reach Baddeck soon enough, if we could cling to that wagon-seat. The morning sun was hot. The way was so uninteresting that we almost wished ourselves back in Nova Scotia. The sandy road was bordered with discouraged evergreens, through which we had glimpses of sand-drifted farms. If Baddeck was to be like this, we had come on a fool's errand. There were some savage, low hills, and the Judique Mountain showed itself as we got away from the town. In this first stage, the heat of the sun, the monotony of the road, and the scarcity of sleep during the past thirty-six hours were all unfavorable to our keeping on the wagon-seat. We nodded separately, we nodded and reeled in unison. But asleep or awake, the driver drove like a son of Jehu. Such driving is the fashion on Cape Breton Island. Especially downhill, we made the most of it; if the horse was on a run, that was only an inducement to apply the lash; speed gave the promise of greater possible speed. The wagon rattled like a bark-mill; it swirled and leaped about, and we finally got the exciting impression that if the whole thing went to pieces, we should somehow go on,--such was our impetus. Round corners, over ruts and stones, and uphill and down, we went jolting and swinging, holding fast to the seat, and putting our trust in things in general. At the end of fifteen miles, we stopped at a Scotch farmhouse, where the driver kept a relay, and changed horse.

The people were Highlanders, and spoke little English; we had struck the beginning of the Gaelic settlement. From here to Hogamah we should encounter only the Gaelic tongue; the inhabitants are all Catholics. Very civil people, apparently, and living in a kind of niggardly thrift, such as the cold land affords. We saw of this family the old man, who had come from Scotland fifty years ago, his stalwart son, six feet and a half high, maybe, and two buxom daughters, going to the hay-field,- -good solid Scotch lassies, who smiled in English, but spoke only Gaelic. The old man could speak a little English, and was disposed to be both communicative and inquisitive. He asked our business, names, and residence. Of the United States he had only a dim conception, but his mind rather rested upon the statement that we lived "near Boston." He complained of the degeneracy of the times. All the young men had gone away from Cape Breton; might get rich if they would stay and work the farms. But no one liked to work nowadays. From life, we diverted the talk to literature. We inquired what books they had.

"Of course you all have the poems of Burns?"

"What's the name o' the mon?"

"Burns, Robert Burns."

"Never heard tell of such a mon. Have heard of Robert Bruce. He was a Scotch-man."

This was nothing short of refreshing, to find a Scotchman who had never heard of Robert Burns! It was worth the whole journey to take this honest man by the hand. How far would I not travel to talk with an American who had never heard of George Washington!

The way was more varied during the next stage; we passed through some pleas-ant valleys and picturesque neighborhoods, and at length, winding around the base of a wooded range, and crossing its point, we came upon a sight that took all the sleep out of us. This was the famous Bras d'Or.

The Bras d'Or is the most beautiful salt-water lake I have ever seen, and more beautiful than we had imagined a body of salt water could be. If the reader will take the map, he will see that two narrow estuaries, the Great and the Little Bras d'Or, enter the island of Cape Breton, on the ragged northeast coast, above the town of Sydney, and flow in, at length widening out and occupying the heart of the island. The water seeks out all the low places, and ramifies the interior, running away into lovely bays and lagoons, leaving slender tongues of land and picturesque islands, and bringing into the recesses of the land, to the remote country farms and settlements, the flavor of salt, and the fish and mollusks of the briny sea. There is very little tide at any time, so that the shores are clean and sightly for the most part, like those of fresh-water lakes. It has all the pleasantness of a fresh-water lake, with all the advantages of a salt one. In the streams which run into it are the speckled trout, the shad, and the salmon; out of its depths are hooked the cod and the mackerel, and in its bays fattens the oyster. This irregular lake is about a hundred miles long, if you measure it skillfully, and in some places ten miles broad; but so indented is it, that I am not sure but one would need, as we were informed, to ride a thousand miles to go round it, following all its incursions into the land. The hills about it are never more than five or six hundred feet high, but they are high enough for reposeful beauty, and offer everywhere pleasing lines.

What we first saw was an inlet of the Bras d'Or, called, by the driver, Hogamah Bay. At its entrance were long, wooded islands, beyond which we saw the backs of graceful hills, like the capes of some poetic sea-coast. The bay narrowed to a mile in width where we came upon it, and ran several miles inland to a swamp, round the head of which we must go. Opposite was the village of Hogamah. I had my suspicions from the beginning about this name, and now asked the driver, who was liberally educated for a driver, how he spelled "Hogamah."

"Why-ko-ko-magh. Hogamah."

Sometimes it is called Wykogamah. Thus the innocent traveler is misled. Along the Whykokomagh Bay we come to a permanent encampment of the Micmac Indians,--a dozen wigwams in the pine woods. Though lumber is plenty, they refuse to live in houses. The wigwams, however, are more picturesque than the square frame houses of the whites. Built up conically of poles, with a hole in the top for the smoke to escape, and often set up a little from the ground on a timber foundation, they are as pleasing to the eye as a Chinese or Turkish dwelling. They may be cold in winter, but blessed be the tenacity of barbarism, which retains this agreeable architecture. The men live by hunting in the season, and the women support the family by making moccasins and baskets. These Indians are most of them good Catholics, and they try to go once a year to mass and a sort of religious festival held at St. Peter's, where their sins are forgiven in a yearly lump.

At Whykokomagh, a neat fishing village of white houses, we stopped for dinner at the Inverness House. The house was very clean, and the tidy landlady gave us as good a dinner as she could of the inevitable green tea, toast, and salt fish. She was Gaelic, but Protestant, as the village is, and showed us with pride her Gaelic Bible and hymn-book. A peaceful place, this Whykokomagh; the lapsing waters of Bras d'Or made a summer music all along the quiet street; the bay lay smiling with its islands in front, and an amphitheater of hills rose behind. But for the line of telegraph poles one might have fancied he could have security and repose here.

We put a fresh pony into the shafts, a beast born with an everlasting uneasiness in his legs, and an amount of "go" in him which suited his reckless driver. We no longer stood upon the order of our going; we went. As we left the village, we passed a rocky hay-field, where the Gaelic farmer was gathering the scanty yield of grass. A comely Indian girl was stowing the hay and treading it down on the wagon. The driver hailed the farmer, and they exchanged Gaelic repartee which set all the hay-makers in a roar, and caused the Indian maid to darkly and sweetly beam upon us. We asked the driver what he had said. He had only inquired what the man would take for the load--as it stood! A joke is a joke down this way.

I am not about to describe this drive at length, in order that the reader may skip it; for I know the reader, being of like passion and fashion with him. From the time we first struck the Bras d'Or for thirty miles we rode in constant sight of its magnificent water. Now we were two hundred feet above the water, on the hillside, skirting a point or following an indentation; and now we were diving into a narrow valley, crossing a stream, or turning a sharp corner, but always with the Bras d'Or in view, the afternoon sun shining on it, softening the outlines of its embracing hills, casting a shadow from its wooded islands. Sometimes we opened on a broad water plain bounded by the Watchabaktchkt hills, and again we looked over hill after hill receding into the soft and hazy blue of the land beyond the great mass of the Bras d'Or. The reader can compare the view and the ride to the Bay of Naples and the Cornice Road; we did nothing of the sort; we held on to the seat, prayed that the harness of the pony might not break, and gave constant expression to our wonder and delight. For a week we had schooled ourselves to expect nothing more from this wicked world, but here was an enchanting vision.

The only phenomenon worthy the attention of any inquiring mind, in this whole record, I will now describe. As we drove along the side of a hill, and at least two hundred feet above the water, the road suddenly diverged and took a circuit higher up. The driver said that was to avoid a sink-hole in the old road,--a great curiosity, which it was worth while to examine. Beside the old road was a circular hole, which nipped out a part of the road-bed, some twenty-five feet in diameter, filled with water almost to the brim, but not running over. The water was dark in color, and I fancied had a brackish taste. The driver said that a few weeks before, when he came this way, it was solid ground where this well now opened, and that a large beech-tree stood there. When he returned next day, he found this hole full of water, as we saw it, and the large tree had sunk in it. The size of the hole seemed to be determined by the reach of the roots of the tree. The tree had so entirely disappeared, that he could not with a long pole touch its top. Since then the water had neither subsided nor overflowed. The ground about was compact gravel. We tried sounding the hole with poles, but could make nothing of it. The water seemed to have no outlet nor inlet; at least, it did not rise or fall. Why should the solid hill give way at this place, and swallow up a tree? and if the water had any connection with the lake, two hundred feet below and at some distance away, why didn't the water run out? Why should the unscientific traveler have a thing of this kind thrown in his way? The driver did not know.

This phenomenon made us a little suspicious of the foundations of this island which is already invaded by the jealous ocean, and is anchored to the continent only by the cable.

The drive became more charming as the sun went down, and we saw the hills grow purple beyond the Bras d'Or. The road wound around lovely coves and across low promontories, giving us new beauties at every turn. Before dark we had crossed the Middle River and the Big Baddeck, on long wooden bridges, which straggled over sluggish waters and long reaches of marsh, upon which Mary might have been sent to call the cattle home. These bridges were shaky and wanted a plank at intervals, but they are in keeping with the enterprise of the country. As dusk came on, we crossed the last hill, and were bowling along by the still gleaming water. Lights began to appear in infrequent farmhouses, and under cover of the gathering night the houses seemed to be stately mansions; and we fancied we were on a noble highway, lined with elegant suburban seaside residences, and about to drive into a town of wealth and a port of great commerce. We were, nevertheless, anxious about Baddeck. What sort of haven were we to reach after our heroic (with the reader's permission) week of travel? Would the hotel be like that at Plaster Cove? Were our thirty-six hours of sleepless staging to terminate in a night of misery and a Sunday of discomfort?

We came into a straggling village; that we could see by the starlight. But we stopped at the door of a very unhotel-like appearing hotel. It had in front a flower-garden; it was blazing with welcome lights; it opened hospitable doors, and we were received by a family who expected us. The house was a large one, for two guests; and we enjoyed the luxury of spacious rooms, an abundant supper, and a friendly welcome; and, in short, found ourselves at home. The proprietor of the Telegraph House is the superintendent of the land lines of Cape Breton, a Scotchman, of course; but his wife is a Newfoundland lady. We cannot violate the sanctity of what seemed like private hospitality by speaking freely of this lady and the lovely girls, her daughters, whose education has been so admirably advanced in the excellent school at Baddeck; but we can confidently advise any American who is going to Newfoundland, to get a wife there, if he wants one at all. It is the only new article he can bring from the Provinces that he will not have to pay duty on. And here is a suggestion to our tariff-mongers for the "protection" of New England women.

The reader probably cannot appreciate the delicious sense of rest and of achievement which we enjoyed in this tidy inn, nor share the anticipations of undisturbed, luxurious sleep, in which we indulged as we sat upon the upper balcony after supper, and saw the moon rise over the glistening Bras d'Or and flood with light the islands and headlands of the beautiful bay. Anchored at some distance from the shore was a slender coasting vessel. The big red moon happened to come up just behind it, and the masts and spars and ropes of the vessel came out, distinctly traced on the golden background, making such a night picture as I once saw painted of a ship in a fiord of Norway. The scene was enchanting. And we respected then the heretofore seemingly insane impulse that had driven us on to Baddeck.

IV

Although it was an open and flagrant violation of the Sabbath day as it is kept in Scotch Baddeck, our kind hosts let us sleep late on Sunday morning, with no reminder that we were not sleeping the sleep of the just. It was the charming Maud, a flitting sunbeam of a girl, who waited to bring us our breakfast, and thereby lost the opportunity of going to church with the rest of the family,--an act of gracious hospitality which the tired travelers appreciated.

The travelers were unable, indeed, to awaken into any feeling of Sabbatical straitness. The morning was delicious,--such a morning as never visits any place except an island; a bright, sparkling morning, with the exhilaration of the air softened by the sea. What a day it was for idleness, for voluptuous rest, after the flight by day and night from St. John! It was enough, now that the morning was fully opened and advancing to the splendor of noon, to sit upon the upper balcony, looking upon the Bras d'Or and the peaceful hills beyond, reposeful and yet sparkling with the air and color of summer, and inhale the balmy air. (We greatly need another word to describe good air, properly heated, besides this overworked "balmy.") Perhaps it might in some regions be considered Sabbath-keeping, simply to rest in such a soothing situation,--rest, and not incessant activity, having been one of the original designs of the day.

But our travelers were from New England, and they were not willing to be out-done in the matter of Sunday observances by such an out-of-the-way and nameless place as Baddeck. They did not set themselves up as missionaries to these benighted Gaelic people, to teach them by example that the notion of Sunday which obtained two hundred years ago in Scotland had been modified, and that the sacredness of it had pretty much disappeared with the unpleasantness of it. They rather lent them-selves to the humor of the hour, and probably by their demeanor encouraged the respect for the day on Cape Breton Island. Neither by birth nor education were the travelers fishermen on Sunday, and they were not moved to tempt the authorities to lock them up for dropping here a line and there a line on the Lord's day.

In fact, before I had finished my second cup of Maud-mixed coffee, my com-panion, with a little show of haste, had gone in search of the kirk, and I followed him, with more scrupulousness, as soon as I could without breaking the day of rest. Although it was Sunday, I could not but notice that Baddeck was a clean-looking village of white wooden houses, of perhaps seven or eight hundred inhabitants; that it stretched along the bay for a mile or more, straggling off into farmhouses at each end, lying for the most part on the sloping curve of the bay. There were a few country-looking stores and shops, and on the shore three or four rather decayed and shaky wharves ran into the water, and a few schooners lay at anchor near them; and the usual decaying warehouses leaned about the docks. A peaceful and perhaps a thriving place, but not a bustling place. As I walked down the road, a sailboat put out from the shore and slowly disappeared round the island in the direction of the Grand Narrows. It had a small pleasure party on board. None of them were drowned that day, and I learned at night that they were Roman Catholics from Whykokornagh.

The kirk, which stands near the water, and at a distance shows a pretty wooden spire, is after the pattern of a New England meeting-house. When I reached it, the house was full and the service had begun. There was something familiar in the bare-ness and uncompromising plainness and ugliness of the interior. The pews had high backs, with narrow, uncushioned seats. The pulpit was high,--a sort of theological fortification,--approached by wide, curving flights of stairs on either side. Those who occupied the near seats to the right and left of the pulpit had in front of them a blank board partition, and could not by any possibility see the minister, though they broke their necks backwards over their high coat-collars. The congregation had a striking resemblance to a country New England congregation of say twenty years ago. The clothes they wore had been Sunday clothes for at least that length of time.

Such clothes have a look of I know not what devout and painful respectability, that is in keeping with the worldly notion of rigid Scotch Presbyterianism. One saw with pleasure the fresh and rosy-cheeked children of this strict generation, but the women of the audience were not in appearance different from newly arrived and respectable Irish immigrants. They wore a white cap with long frills over the forehead, and a black handkerchief thrown over it and hanging down the neck,--a quaint and not unpleasing disguise.

The house, as I said, was crowded. It is the custom in this region to go to church,--for whole families to go, even the smallest children; and they not unfrequently walk six or seven miles to attend the service. There is a kind of merit in this act that makes up for the lack of certain other Christian virtues that are practiced elsewhere. The service was worth coming seven miles to participate in!--it was about two hours long, and one might well feel as if he had performed a work of long-suffering to sit through it. The singing was strictly congregational. Congregational singing is good (for those who like it) when the congregation can sing. This congregation could not sing, but it could grind the Psalms of David powerfully. They sing nothing else but the old Scotch version of the Psalms, in a patient and faithful long meter. And this is regarded, and with considerable plausibility, as an act of worship. It certainly has small element of pleasure in it. Here is a stanza from Psalm xlv., which the congregation, without any instrumental nonsense, went through in a dragging, drawling manner, and with perfect individual independence as to time:

"Thine arrows sharply pierce the heart of th' enemies of the king, And under thy sub-jec-shi-on the people down do bring."

The sermon was extempore, and in English with Scotch pronunciation; and it filled a solid hour of time. I am not a good judge of sermons, and this one was mere chips to me; but my companion, who knows a sermon when he hears it, said that this was strictly theological, and Scotch theology at that, and not at all expository. It was doubtless my fault that I got no idea whatever from it. But the adults of the congregation appeared to be perfectly satisfied with it; at least they sat bolt upright and nodded assent continually. The children all went to sleep under it, without any hypocritical show of attention. To be sure, the day was warm and the house was unventilated. If the windows had been opened so as to admit the fresh air from the Bras d'Or, I presume the hard-working farmers and their wives would have resented such an interference with their ordained Sunday naps, and the preacher's sermon would have seemed more musty than it appeared to be in that congenial and drowsy air. Considering that only half of the congregation could understand the preacher, its behavior was exemplary.

After the sermon, a collection was taken up for the minister; and I noticed that nothing but pennies rattled into the boxes,--a melancholy sound for the pastor. This might appear niggardly on the part of these Scotch Presbyterians, but it is on principle that they put only a penny into the box; they say that they want a free gospel, and so far as they are concerned they have it. Although the farmers about the Bras d'Or are well-to-do they do not give their minister enough to keep his soul in his Gaelic body, and his poor support is eked out by the contributions of a missionary society. It was gratifying to learn that this was not from stinginess on the part of the people, but was due to their religious principle. It seemed to us that everybody ought to be good in a country where it costs next to nothing.

When the service was over, about half of the people departed; the rest remained in their seats and prepared to enter upon their Sabbath exercises. These latter were all Gaelic people, who had understood little or nothing of the English service. The minister turned himself at once into a Gaelic preacher and repeated in that language the long exercises of the morning. The sermon and perhaps the prayers were quite as enjoyable in Gaelic as in English, and the singing was a great improvement. It was of the same Psalms, but the congregation chanted them in a wild and weird tone and manner, as wailing and barbarous to modern ears as any Highland devotional outburst of two centuries ago. This service also lasted about two hours; and as soon as it was over the faithful minister, without any rest or refreshment, organized the Sunday-school, and it must have been half past three o'clock before that was over. And this is considered a day of rest.

These Gaelic Christians, we were informed, are of a very old pattern; and some of them cling more closely to religious observances than to morality. Sunday is nowhere observed with more strictness. The community seems to be a very orderly and thrifty one, except upon solemn and stated occasions. One of these occasions is the celebration of the Lord's Supper; and in this the ancient Highland traditions are preserved. The rite is celebrated not oftener than once a year by any church. It then invites the neighboring churches to partake with it,--the celebration being usually in the summer and early fall months. It has some of the characteristics of a "camp-meeting." People come from long distances, and as many as two thousand and three thousand assemble together. They quarter themselves without special invitation upon the members of the inviting church. Sometimes fifty people will pounce upon one farmer, overflowing his house and his barn and swarming all about his premises, consuming all the provisions he has laid up for his family, and all he can raise money to buy, and literally eating him out of house and home. Not seldom a man is almost ruined by one of these religious raids,--at least he is left with a debt of hundreds of dollars. The multitude assembles on Thursday and remains over Sunday. There is preaching every day, but there is something besides. Whatever may be the devotion of a part of the assembly, the four days are, in general, days of license, of carousing, of drinking, and of other excesses, which our informant said he would not particularize; we could understand what they were by reading St. Paul's rebuke of the Corinthians for similar offenses. The evil has become so great and burdensome that the celebration of this sacred rite will have to be reformed altogether.

Such a Sabbath quiet pervaded the street of Baddeck, that the fast driving of the Gaels in their rattling, one-horse wagons, crowded full of men, women, and children,--released from their long sanctuary privileges, and going home,--was a sort of profanation of the day; and we gladly turned aside to visit the rural jail of the town.

Upon the principal street or road of Baddeck stands the dreadful prison-house. It is a story and a quarter edifice, built of stone and substantially whitewashed; retired a little from the road, with a square of green turf in front of it, I should have taken it for the residence of the Dairyman's Daughter, but for the iron gratings at the lower windows. A more inviting place to spend the summer in, a vicious person could not have. The Scotch keeper of it is an old, garrulous, obliging man, and keeps codfish tackle to loan. I think that if he had a prisoner who was fond of fishing, he would take him with him on the bay in pursuit of the mackerel and the cod. If the prisoner were to take advantage of his freedom and attempt to escape, the jailer's feelings would be hurt, and public opinion would hardly approve the prisoner's conduct.

The jail door was hospitably open, and the keeper invited us to enter. Having seen the inside of a good many prisons in our own country (officially), we were interested in inspecting this. It was a favorable time for doing so, for there happened to be a man confined there, a circumstance which seemed to increase the keeper's feeling of responsibility in his office. The edifice had four rooms on the ground-floor, and an attic sleeping-room above. Three of these rooms, which were perhaps twelve feet by fifteen feet, were cells; the third was occupied by the jailer's family. The family were now also occupying the front cell,--a cheerful room commanding a view of the village street and of the bay. A prisoner of a philosophic turn of mind, who had committed some crime of sufficient magnitude to make him willing to retire from the world for a season and rest, might enjoy himself here very well.

The jailer exhibited his premises with an air of modesty. In the rear was a small yard, surrounded by a board fence, in which the prisoner took his exercise. An active boy could climb over it, and an enterprising pig could go through it almost anywhere. The keeper said that he intended at the next court to ask the commissioners to build the fence higher and stop up the holes. Otherwise the jail was in good condition. Its inmates were few; in fact, it was rather apt to be empty: its occupants were usually prisoners for debt, or for some trifling breach of the peace, committed under the influence of the liquor that makes one "unco happy." Whether or not the people of the region have a high moral standard, crime is almost unknown; the jail itself is an evidence of primeval simplicity. The great incident in the old jailer's life had been the rescue of a well-known citizen who was confined on a charge of misuse of public money. The keeper showed me a place in the outer wall of the front cell, where an attempt had been made to batter a hole through. The Highland clan and kinsfolk of the alleged defaulter came one night and threatened to knock the jail in pieces if he was not given up. They bruised the wall, broke the windows, and finally smashed in the door and took their man away. The jailer was greatly excited at this rudeness, and went almost immediately and purchased a pistol. He said that for a time he did n't feel safe in the jail without it. The mob had thrown stones at the upper windows, in order to awaken him, and had insulted him with cursing and offensive language.

Having finished inspecting the building, I was unfortunately moved by I know not what national pride and knowledge of institutions superior to this at home, to say,

"This is a pleasant jail, but it doesn't look much like our great prisons; we have as many as a thousand to twelve hundred men in some of our institutions."

"Ay, ay, I have heard tell," said the jailer, shaking his head in pity, "it's an awfu' place, an awfu' place,--the United States. I suppose it's the wickedest country that ever was in the world. I don't know,--I don't know what is to become of it. It's worse than Sodom. There was that dreadful war on the South; and I hear now it's very unsafe, full of murders and robberies and corruption."

I did not attempt to correct this impression concerning my native land, for I saw it was a comfort to the simple jailer, but I tried to put a thorn into him by saying,

"Yes, we have a good many criminals, but the majority of them, the majority of those in jails, are foreigners; they come from Ireland, England, and the Provinces."

But the old man only shook his head more solemnly, and persisted, "It's an awfu' wicked country."

Before I came away I was permitted to have an interview with the sole prisoner, a very pleasant and talkative man, who was glad to see company, especially intelligent company who understood about things, he was pleased to say. I have seldom met a more agreeable rogue, or one so philosophical, a man of travel and varied experiences. He was a lively, robust Provincial of middle age, bullet-headed, with a mass of curly black hair, and small, round black eyes, that danced and sparkled with good humor. He was by trade a carpenter, and had a work-bench in his cell, at which he worked on week-days. He had been put in jail on suspicion of stealing a buffalo-robe, and he lay in jail eight months, waiting for the judge to come to Baddeck on his yearly circuit. He did not steal the robe, as he assured me, but it was found in his house, and the judge gave him four months in jail, making a year in all,--a month of which was still to serve. But he was not at all anxious for the end of his term; for his wife was outside.

Jock, for he was familiarly so called, asked me where I was from. As I had not found it very profitable to hail from the United States, and had found, in fact, that the name United States did not convey any definite impression to the average Cape

Breton mind, I ventured upon the bold assertion, for which I hope Bostonians will forgive me, that I was from Boston. For Boston is known in the eastern Provinces.

"Are you?" cried the man, delighted. "I've lived in Boston, myself. There's just been an awful fire near there."

"Indeed!" I said; "I heard nothing of it.' And I was startled with the possibility that Boston had burned up again while we were crawling along through Nova Scotia.

"Yes, here it is, in the last paper." The man bustled away and found his late paper, and thrust it through the grating, with the inquiry, "Can you read?"

Though the question was unexpected, and I had never thought before whether I could read or not, I confessed that I could probably make out the meaning, and took the newspaper. The report of the fire "near Boston" turned out to be the old news of the conflagration in Portland, Oregon!

Disposed to devote a portion of this Sunday to the reformation of this lively criminal, I continued the conversation with him. It seemed that he had been in jail before, and was not unaccustomed to the life. He was not often lonesome; he had his workbench and newspapers, and it was a quiet place; on the whole, he enjoyed it, and should rather regret it when his time was up, a month from then.

Had he any family?

"Oh, yes. When the census was round, I contributed more to it than anybody in town. Got a wife and eleven children."

"Well, don't you think it would pay best to be honest, and live with your family, out of jail? You surely never had anything but trouble from dishonesty."

"That's about so, boss. I mean to go on the square after this. But, you see," and here he began to speak confidentially, "things are fixed about so in this world, and a man's got to live his life. I tell you how it was. It all came about from a woman. I was a carpenter, had a good trade, and went down to St. Peter's to work. There I got acquainted with a Frenchwoman,--you know what Frenchwomen are,--and I had to marry her. The fact is, she was rather low family; not so very low, you know, but not so good as mine. Well, I wanted to go to Boston to work at my trade, but she wouldn't go; and I went, but she would n't come to me, so in two or three years I came back. A man can't help himself, you know, when he gets in with a woman, especially a Frenchwoman. Things did n't go very well, and never have. I can't make much out of it, but I reckon a man 's got to live his life. Ain't that about so?"

"Perhaps so. But you'd better try to mend matters when you get out. Won't it seem rather good to get out and see your wife and family again?"

"I don't know. I have peace here."

The question of his liberty seemed rather to depress this cheerful and vivacious philosopher, and I wondered what the woman could be from whose companionship the man chose to be protected by jail-bolts. I asked the landlord about her, and his reply was descriptive and sufficient. He only said,

"She's a yelper."

Besides the church and the jail there are no public institutions in Baddeck to see on Sunday, or on any other day; but it has very good schools, and the examination-papers of Maud and her elder sister would do credit to Boston scholars even. You would not say that the place was stuffed with books, or overrun by lecturers, but it is an orderly, Sabbath-keeping, fairly intelligent town. Book-agents visit it with other commercial travelers, but the flood of knowledge, which is said to be the beginning of sorrow, is hardly turned in that direction yet. I heard of a feeble lecture-course in Halifax, supplied by local celebrities, some of them from St. John; but so far as I can see, this is a virgin field for the platform philosophers under whose instructions we have become the well-informed people we are.

The peaceful jail and the somewhat tiresome church exhaust one's opportunities for doing good in Baddeck on Sunday. There seemed to be no idlers about, to reprove; the occasional lounger on the skeleton wharves was in his Sunday clothes, and therefore within the statute. No one, probably, would have thought of rowing out beyond the island to fish for cod,--although, as that fish is ready to bite, and his associations are more or less sacred, there might be excuses for angling for him on Sunday, when it would be wicked to throw a line for another sort of fish. My earliest recollections are of the codfish on the meeting-house spires in New England,--his sacred tail pointing the way the wind went. I did not know then why this emblem should be placed upon a house of worship, any more than I knew why codfish-balls appeared always upon the Sunday breakfast-table. But these associations invested this plebeian fish with something of a religious character, which he has never quite lost, in my mind.

Having attributed the quiet of Baddeck on Sunday to religion, we did not know to what to lay the quiet on Monday. But its peacefulness continued. I have no doubt that the farmers began to farm, and the traders to trade, and the sailors to sail; but the tourist felt that he had come into a place of rest. The promise of the red sky the evening before was fulfilled in another royal day. There was an inspiration in the air that one looks for rather in the mountains than on the sea-coast; it seemed like some new and gentle compound of sea-air and land-air, which was the perfection of breathing material. In this atmosphere, which seemed to flow over all these Atlantic isles at this season, one endures a great deal of exertion with little fatigue; or he is content to sit still, and has no feeling of sluggishness. Mere living is a kind of happiness, and the easy-going traveler is satisfied with little to do and less to see, Let the reader not understand that we are recommending him to go to Baddeck. Far from it. The reader was never yet advised to go to any place, which he did not growl about if he took the advice and went there. If he discovers it himself, the case is different. We know too well what would happen. A shoal of travelers would pour down upon Cape Breton, taking with them their dyspepsia, their liver-complaints, their "lights" derangements, their discontent, their guns and fishing-tackle, their big trunks, their desire for rapid travel, their enthusiasm about the Gaelic language, their love for nature; and they would very likely declare that there was nothing in it. And the traveler would probably be right, so far as he is concerned. There are few whom it would pay to go a thousand miles for the sake of sitting on the dock at Baddeck when the sun goes down, and watching the purple lights on the islands and the distant hills, the red flush in the horizon and on the lake, and the creeping on of gray twilight. You can see all that as well elsewhere? I am not so sure. There is a harmony of beauty about the Bras d'Or at Baddeck which is lacking in many scenes of more pretension. No. We advise no person to go to Cape Breton. But if any one does go, he need not lack occupation. If he is there late in the fall or early in the winter, he may hunt, with good luck, if he is able to hit anything with a rifle, the moose and the caribou on that long wilderness peninsula between Baddeck and Aspy Bay, where the old cable landed. He may also have his fill of salmon fishing in June and July, especially on the Matjorie River. As late as August, at the time, of our visit, a hundred people were camped in tents on the Marjorie, wiling the salmon with the delusive fly, and leading him to death with a hook in his nose. The speckled trout lives in all the streams, and can be caught whenever he will bite. The day we went for him appeared to be an off-day, a sort of holiday with him.

There is one place, however, which the traveler must not fail to visit. That is St. Ann's Bay. He will go light of baggage, for he must hire a farmer to carry him from the Bras d'Or to the branch of St. Ann's harbor, and a part of his journey will be in a row-boat. There is no ride on the continent, of the kind, so full of picturesque beauty and constant surprises as this around the indentations of St. Ann's harbor. From the high promontory where rests the fishing village of St. Ann, the traveler will cross to English Town. High bluffs, bold shores, exquisite sea-views, mountain-ous ranges, delicious air, the society of a member of the Dominion Parliament, these are some of the things to be enjoyed at this place. In point of grandeur and beauty it surpasses Mt. Desert, and is really the most attractive place on the whole line of the Atlantic Cable. If the traveler has any sentiment in him, he will visit here, not without emotion, the grave of the Nova Scotia Giant, who recently laid his huge frame along this, his native shore. A man of gigantic height and awful breadth of shoulders, with a hand as big as a shovel, there was nothing mean or little in his soul. While the visitor is gazing at his vast shoes, which now can be used only as sledges, he will be told that the Giant was greatly respected by his neighbors as a man of ability and simple integrity. He was not spoiled by his metropolitan success-es, bringing home from his foreign triumphs the same quiet and friendly demeanor he took away; he is almost the only example of a successful public man, who did not feel bigger than he was. He performed his duty in life without ostentation, and returned to the home he loved unspoiled by the flattery of constant public curios-ity. He knew, having tried both, how much better it is to be good than to be great. I should like to have known him. I should like to know how the world looked to him from his altitude. I should like to know how much food it took at one time to make an impression on him; I should like to know what effect an idea of ordinary size had in his capacious head. I should like to feel that thrill of physical delight he must have experienced in merely closing his hand over something. It is a pity that he could not have been educated all through, beginning at a high school, and end-ing in a university. There was a field for the multifarious new education! If we could have annexed him with his island, I should like to have seen him in the Senate of the United States. He would have made foreign nations respect that body, and fear his lightest remark like a declaration of war. And he would have been at home in that body of great men. Alas! he has passed away, leaving little influence except a good example of growth, and a grave which is a new promontory on that ragged coast swept by the winds of the untamed Atlantic.

I could describe the Bay of St. Ann more minutely and graphically, if it were desirable to do so; but I trust that enough has been said to make the traveler wish to go there. I more unreservedly urge him to go there, because we did not go, and we should feel no responsibility for his liking or disliking. He will go upon the recommendation of two gentlemen of taste and travel whom we met at Baddeck, residents of Maine and familiar with most of the odd and striking combinations of land and water in coast scenery. When a Maine man admits that there is any place finer than Mt. Desert, it is worth making a note of.

On Monday we went a-fishing. Davie hitched to a rattling wagon something that he called a horse, a small, rough animal with a great deal of "go" in him, if he could be coaxed to show it. For the first half-hour he went mostly in a circle in front of the inn, moving indifferently backwards or forwards, perfectly willing to go down the road, but refusing to start along the bay in the direction of Middle River. Of course a crowd collected to give advice and make remarks, and women appeared at the doors and windows of adjacent houses. Davie said he did n't care anything about the conduct of the horse, --he could start him after a while,--but he did n't like to have all the town looking at him, especially the girls; and besides, such an exhibition affected the market value of the horse. We sat in the wagon circling round and round, sometimes in the ditch and sometimes out of it, and Davie "whaled" the horse with his whip and abused him with his tongue. It was a pleasant day, and the spectators increased.

There are two ways of managing a balky horse. My companion knew one of them and I the other. His method is to sit quietly in the wagon, and at short intervals throw a small pebble at the horse. The theory is that these repeated sudden annoyances will operate on a horse's mind, and he will try to escape them by going on. The spectators supplied my friend with stones, and he pelted the horse with measured gentleness. Probably the horse understood this method, for he did not notice the attack at all. My plan was to speak gently to the horse, requesting him to go, and then to follow the refusal by one sudden, sharp cut of the lash; to wait a moment, and then repeat the operation. The dread of the coming lash after the gentle word will start any horse. I tried this, and with a certain success. The horse backed us into the ditch, and would probably have backed himself into the wagon, if I had continued. When the animal was at length ready to go, Davie took him by the bridle, ran by his side, coaxed him into a gallop, and then, leaping in behind, lashed him into a run, which had little respite for ten miles, uphill or down. Remonstrance on behalf of the horse was in vain, and it was only on the return home that this specimen Cape Breton driver began to reflect how he could erase the welts from the horse's back before his father saw them.

Our way lay along the charming bay of the Bras d'Or, over the sprawling bridge of the Big Baddeck, a black, sedgy, lonesome stream, to Middle River, which debouches out of a scraggy country into a bayou with ragged shores, about which the Indians have encampments, and in which are the skeleton stakes of fish-weirs. Saturday night we had seen trout jumping in the still water above the bridge. We followed the stream up two or three miles to a Gaelic settlement of farmers. The river here flows through lovely meadows, sandy, fertile, and sheltered by hills,--a green Eden, one of the few peaceful inhabited spots in the world. I could conceive of no news coming to these Highlanders later than the defeat of the Pretender. Turning from the road, through a lane and crossing a shallow brook, we reached the dwelling of one of the original McGregors, or at least as good as an original. Mr. McGregor is a fiery-haired Scotchman and brother, cordial and hospitable, who entertained our wayward horse, and freely advised us where the trout on his farm were most likely to be found at this season of the year.

It would be a great pleasure to speak well of Mr. McGregor's residence, but truth is older than Scotchmen, and the reader looks to us for truth and not flattery. Though the McGregor seems to have a good farm, his house is little better than a shanty, a rather cheerless place for the "woman" to slave away her uneventful life in, and bring up her scantily clothed and semi-wild flock of children. And yet I suppose there must be happiness in it,--there always is where there are plenty of children, and milk enough for them. A white-haired boy who lacked adequate trousers, small though he was, was brought forward by his mother to describe a trout he had recently caught, which was nearly as long as the boy himself. The young Gael's invention was rewarded by a present of real fish-hooks. We found here in this rude cabin the hospitality that exists in all remote regions where travelers are few. Mrs.

McGregor had none of that reluctance, which women feel in all more civilized ag-
ricultural regions, to "break a pan of milk," and Mr. McGregor even pressed us to
partake freely of that simple drink. And he refused to take any pay for it, in a sort of
surprise that such a simple act of hospitality should have any commercial value. But
travelers themselves destroy one of their chief pleasures. No doubt we planted the
notion in the McGregor mind that the small kindnesses of life may be made profitable, by offering to pay for the milk; and probably the next travelers in that Eden
will succeed in leaving some small change there, if they use a little tact.

It was late in the season for trout. Perhaps the McGregor was aware of that
when he freely gave us the run of the stream in his meadows, and pointed out the
pools where we should be sure of good luck. It was a charming August day, just the
day that trout enjoy lying in cool, deep places, and moving their fins in quiet content, indifferent to the skimming fly or to the proffered sport of rod and reel. The
Middle River gracefully winds through this Vale of Tempe, over a sandy bottom,
sometimes sparkling in shallows, and then gently reposing in the broad bends of
the grassy banks. It was in one of these bends, where the stream swirled around in
seductive eddies, that we tried our skill. We heroically waded the stream and threw
our flies from the highest bank; but neither in the black water nor in the sandy
shallows could any trout be coaxed to spring to the deceitful leaders. We enjoyed
the distinction of being the only persons who had ever failed to strike trout in that
pool, and this was something. The meadows were sweet with the newly cut grass,
the wind softly blew down the river, large white clouds sailed high overhead and
cast shadows on the changing water; but to all these gentle influences the fish were
insensible, and sulked in their cool retreats. At length in a small brook flowing into
the Middle River we found the trout more sociable; and it is lucky that we did so, for
I should with reluctance stain these pages with a fiction; and yet the public would
have just reason to resent a fish-story without any fish in it. Under a bank, in a pool
crossed by a log and shaded by a tree, we found a drove of the speckled beauties
at home, dozens of them a foot long, each moving lazily a little, their black backs
relieved by their colored fins. They must have seen us, but at first they showed no
desire for a closer acquaintance. To the red ibis and the white miller and the brown
hackle and the gray fly they were alike indifferent. Perhaps the love for made flies is
an artificial taste and has to be cultivated. These at any rate were uncivilized -trout,

and it was only when we took the advice of the young McGregor and baited our hooks with the angleworm, that the fish joined in our day's sport. They could not resist the lively wiggle of the worm before their very noses, and we lifted them out one after an other, gently, and very much as if we were hooking them out of a barrel, until we had a handsome string. It may have been fun for them but it was not much sport for us. All the small ones the young McGregor contemptuously threw back into the water. The sportsman will perhaps learn from this incident that there are plenty of trout in Cape Breton in August, but that the fishing is not exhilarating.

The next morning the semi-weekly steamboat from Sydney came into the bay, and drew all the male inhabitants of Baddeck down to the wharf; and the two travelers, reluctant to leave the hospitable inn, and the peaceful jail, and the double-barreled church, and all the loveliness of this reposeful place, prepared to depart. The most conspicuous person on the steamboat was a thin man, whose extraordinary height was made more striking by his very long-waisted black coat and his very short pantaloons. He was so tall that he had a little difficulty in keeping his balance, and his hat was set upon the back of his head to preserve his equilibrium. He had arrived at that stage when people affected as he was are oratorical, and overflowing with information and good-nature. With what might in strict art be called an excess of expletives, he explained that he was a civil engineer, that he had lost his rubber coat, that he was a great traveler in the Provinces, and he seemed to find a humorous satisfaction in reiterating the fact of his familiarity with Painsec junction. It evidently hovered in the misty horizon of his mind as a joke, and he contrived to present it to his audience in that light. From the deck of the steamboat he addressed the town, and then, to the relief of the passengers, he decided to go ashore. When the boat drew away on her voyage we left him swaying perilously near the edge of the wharf, good-naturedly resenting the grasp of his coat-tail by a friend, addressing us upon the topics of the day, and wishing us prosperity and the Fourth of July. His was the only effort in the nature of a public lecture that we heard in the Provinces, and we could not judge of his ability without hearing a "course."

Perhaps it needed this slight disturbance, and the contrast of this hazy mind with the serene clarity of the day, to put us into the most complete enjoyment of our voyage. Certainly, as we glided out upon the summer waters and began to get the graceful outlines of the widening shores, it seemed as if we had taken passage to the Fortunate Islands.

V

"One town, one country, is very like another; ...... there are indeed minute discriminations both of places and manners, which, perhaps, are not wanting of curiosity, but which a traveller seldom stays long enough to investigate and compare."

--DR. JOHNSON.

There was no prospect of any excitement or of any adventure on the steamboat from Baddeck to West Bay, the southern point of the Bras d'Or. Judging from the appearance of the boat, the dinner might have been an experiment, but we ran no risks. It was enough to sit on deck forward of the wheel-house, and absorb, by all the senses, the delicious day. With such weather perpetual and such scenery always present, sin in this world would soon become an impossibility. Even towards the passengers from Sydney, with their imitation English ways and little insular gossip, one could have only charity and the most kindly feeling.

The most electric American, heir of all the nervous diseases of all the ages, could not but find peace in this scene of tranquil beauty, and sail on into a great and deepening contentment. Would the voyage could last for an age, with the same sparkling but tranquil sea, and the same environment of hills, near and remote! The hills approached and fell away in lines of undulating grace, draped with a tender color which helped to carry the imagination beyond the earth. At this point the narrative needs to flow into verse, but my comrade did not feel like another attempt at poetry so soon after that on the Gut of Canso. A man cannot always be keyed up to the pitch of production, though his emotions may be highly creditable to him. But poetry-making in these days is a good deal like the use of profane language,--

often without the least provocation.

Twelve miles from Baddeck we passed through the Barra Strait, or the Grand Narrows, a picturesque feature in the Bras d'Or, and came into its widest expanse. At the Narrows is a small settlement with a flag-staff and a hotel, and roads leading to farmhouses on the hills. Here is a Catholic chapel; and on shore a fat padre was waiting in his wagon for the inevitable priest we always set ashore at such a place. The missionary we landed was the young father from Arichat, and in appearance the pleasing historical Jesuit. Slender is too corpulent a word to describe his thinness, and his stature was primeval. Enveloped in a black coat, the skirts of which reached his heels, and surmounted by a black hat with an enormous brim, he had the form of an elegant toadstool. The traveler is always grateful for such figures, and is not disposed to quarrel with the faith which preserves so much of the ugly picturesque. A peaceful farming country this, but an unremunerative field, one would say, for the colporteur and the book-agent; and winter must inclose it in a lonesome seclusion.

The only other thing of note the Bras d'Or offered us before we reached West Bay was the finest show of medusm or jelly-fish that could be produced. At first there were dozens of these disk-shaped, transparent creatures, and then hundreds, starring the water like marguerites sprinkled on a meadow, and of sizes from that of a teacup to a dinner-plate. We soon ran into a school of them, a convention, a herd as extensive as the vast buffalo droves on the plains, a collection as thick as clover-blossoms in a field in June, miles of them, apparently; and at length the boat had to push its way through a mass of them which covered the water like the leaves of the pondlily, and filled the deeps far down with their beautiful contracting and expanding forms. I did not suppose there were so many jelly-fishes in all the world. What a repast they would have made for the Atlantic whale we did not see, and what inward comfort it would have given him to have swum through them once or twice with open mouth! Our delight in this wondrous spectacle did not prevent this generous wish for the gratification of the whale. It is probably a natural human desire to see big corporations swallow up little ones.

At the West Bay landing, where there is nothing whatever attractive, we found a great concourse of country wagons and clamorous drivers, to transport the passengers over the rough and uninteresting nine miles to Port Hawkesbury. Competition makes the fare low, but nothing makes the ride entertaining. The only settlement passed through has the promising name of River Inhabitants, but we could see little river and less inhabitants; country and people seem to belong to that commonplace order out of which the traveler can extract nothing amusing, instructive, or disagreeable; and it was a great relief when we came over the last hill and looked down upon the straggling village of Port Hawkesbury and the winding Gut of Canso.

One cannot but feel a respect for this historical strait, on account of the protection it once gave our British ancestors. Smollett makes a certain Captain C----tell this anecdote of George II. and his enlightened minister, the Duke of Newcastle: "In the beginning of the war this poor, half-witted creature told me, in a great fright, that thirty thousand French had marched from Acadie to Cape Breton. 'Where did they find transports?' said I. 'Transports!' cried he; 'I tell you, they marched by land.' By land to the island of Cape Breton?' 'What! is Cape Breton an island?' 'Certainly.' 'Ha! are you sure of that?' When I pointed it out on the map, he examined it earnestly with his spectacles; then taking me in his arms, 'My dear C----!' cried he, you always bring us good news. I'll go directly and tell the king that Cape Breton is an island.'"

Port Hawkesbury is not a modern settlement, and its public house is one of the irregular, old-fashioned, stuffy taverns, with low rooms, chintz-covered lounges, and fat-cushioned rocking-chairs, the decay and untidiness of which are not offensive to the traveler. It has a low back porch looking towards the water and over a mouldy garden, damp and unseemly. Time was, no doubt, before the rush of travel rubbed off the bloom of its ancient hospitality and set a vigilant man at the door of the dining-room to collect pay for meals, that this was an abode of comfort and the resort of merry-making and frolicsome provincials. On this now decaying porch no doubt lovers sat in the moonlight, and vowed by the Gut of Canso to be fond of each other forever. The traveler cannot help it if he comes upon the traces of such sentiment. There lingered yet in the house an air of the hospitable old time; the swift willingness of the waiting-maids at table, who were eager that we should miss none of the home-made dishes, spoke of it; and as we were not obliged to stay in the hotel and lodge in its six-by-four bedrooms, we could afford to make a little romance about its history.

While we were at supper the steamboat arrived from Pictou. We hastened on board, impatient for progress on our homeward journey. But haste was not called for. The steamboat would not sail on her return till morning. No one could tell why. It was not on account of freight to take in or discharge; it was not in hope of more passengers, for they were all on board. But if the boat had returned that night to Pictou, some of the passengers might have left her and gone west by rail, instead of wasting two, or three days lounging through Northumberland Sound and idling in the harbors of Prince Edward Island. If the steamboat would leave at midnight, we could catch the railway train at Pictou. Probably the officials were aware of this, and they preferred to have our company to Shediac. We mention this so that the tourist who comes this way may learn to possess his soul in patience, and know that steamboats are not run for his accommodation, but to give him repose and to familiarize him with the country. It is almost impossible to give the unscientific reader an idea of the slowness of travel by steamboat in these regions. Let him first fix his mind on the fact that the earth moves through space at a speed of more than sixty-six thousand miles an hour. This is a speed eleven hundred times greater than that of the most rapid express trains. If the distance traversed by a locomotive in an hour is represented by one tenth of an inch, it would need a line nine feet long to indicate the corresponding advance of the earth in the same time. But a tortoise, pursuing his ordinary gait without a wager, moves eleven hundred times slower than an express train. We have here a basis of comparison with the provincial steamboats. If we had seen a tortoise start that night from Port Hawkesbury for the west, we should have desired to send letters by him.

In the early morning we stole out of the romantic strait, and by breakfast-time we were over St. George's Bay and round his cape, and making for the harbor of Pictou. During the forenoon something in the nature of an excursion developed itself on the steamboat, but it had so few of the bustling features of an American excursion that I thought it might be a pilgrimage. Yet it doubtless was a highly developed provincial lark. For a certain portion of the passengers had the unmistakable excursion air: the half-jocular manner towards each other, the local facetiousness which is so offensive to uninterested fellow-travelers, that male obsequiousness about ladies' shawls and reticules, the clumsy pretense of gallantry with each other's wives, the anxiety about the company luggage and the company health. It became painfully evident presently that it was an excursion, for we heard singing of that concerted and determined kind that depresses the spirits of all except those who join in it. The excursion had assembled on the lee guards out of the wind, and was enjoying itself in an abandon of serious musical enthusiasm. We feared at first that there might be some levity in this performance, and that the unrestrained spirit of the excursion was working itself off in social and convivial songs. But it was not so. The singers were provided with hymn-and-tune books, and what they sang they rendered in long meter and with a most doleful earnestness. It is agreeable to the traveler to see that the provincials disport themselves within bounds, and that an hilarious spree here does not differ much in its exercises from a prayer-meeting elsewhere. But the excursion enjoyed its staid dissipation amazingly.

It is pleasant to sail into the long and broad harbor of Pictou on a sunny day. On the left is the Halifax railway terminus, and three rivers flow into the harbor from the south. On the right the town of Pictou, with its four thousand inhabitants, lies upon the side of the ridge that runs out towards the Sound. The most conspicuous building in it as we approach is the Roman Catholic church; advanced to the edge of the town and occupying the highest ground, it appears large, and its gilt cross is a beacon miles away. Its builders understood the value of a striking situation, a dominant position; it is a part of the universal policy of this church to secure the commanding places for its houses of worship. We may have had no prejudices in favor of the Papal temporality when we landed at Pictou, but this church was the only one which impressed us, and the only one we took the trouble to visit. We had ample time, for the steamboat after its arduous trip needed rest, and remained some hours in the harbor. Pictou is said to be a thriving place, and its streets have a cindery appearance, betokening the nearness of coal mines and the presence of furnaces. But the town has rather a cheap and rusty look. Its streets rise one above another on the hillside, and, except a few comfortable cottages, we saw no evidences of wealth in the dwellings. The church, when we reached it, was a commonplace brick structure, with a raw, unfinished interior, and weedy and untidy surroundings, so that our expectation of sitting on the inviting hill and enjoying the view was not realized; and we were obliged to descend to the hot wharf and wait for the ferry-boat to take us to the steamboat which lay at the railway terminus opposite. It is the most unfair thing in the world for the traveler, without an object or any interest in the development of the country, on a sleepy day in August, to express any opinion whatever about such a town as Pictou. But we may say of it, without offence, that it occupies a charming situation, and may have an interesting future; and that a person on a short acquaintance can leave it without regret.

By stopping here we had the misfortune to lose our excursion, a loss that was soothed by no know ledge of its destination or hope of seeing it again, and a loss without a hope is nearly always painful. Going out of the harbor we encounter Pictou Island and Light, and presently see the low coast of Prince Edward Island,--a coast indented and agreeable to those idly sailing along it, in weather that seemed let down out of heaven and over a sea that sparkled but still slept in a summer quiet. When fate puts a man in such a position and relieves him of all responsibility, with a book and a good comrade, and liberty to make sarcastic remarks upon his fellow-travelers, or to doze, or to look over the tranquil sea, he may be pronounced happy. And I believe that my companion, except in the matter of the comrade, was happy. But I could not resist a worrying anxiety about the future of the British Provinces, which not even the remembrance of their hostility to us during our mortal strife with the Rebellion could render agreeable. For I could not but feel that the ostentatious and unconcealable prosperity of "the States" over-shadows this part of the continent. And it was for once in vain that I said, "Have we not a common land and a common literature, and no copyright, and a common pride in Shakespeare and Hannah More and Colonel Newcome and Pepys's Diary?" I never knew this sort of consolation to fail before; it does not seem to answer in the Provinces as well as it does in England.

New passengers had come on board at Pictou, new and hungry, and not all could get seats for dinner at the first table. Notwithstanding the supposed traditionary advantage of our birthplace, we were unable to dispatch this meal with the celerity of our fellow-voyagers, and consequently, while we lingered over our tea, we found ourselves at the second table. And we were rewarded by one of those pleasing sights that go to make up the entertainment of travel. There sat down opposite to us a fat man whose noble proportions occupied at the board the space of three ordinary men. His great face beamed delight the moment he came near the table. He had a low forehead and a wide mouth and small eyes, and an internal capacity that was a prophecy of famine to his fellow-men. But a more good-natured, pleased animal you may never see. Seating himself with unrepressed joy, he looked at us, and a great smile of satisfaction came over his face, that plainly said, "Now my time has come." Every part of his vast bulk said this. Most generously, by his friendly glances, he made us partners in his pleasure. With a Napoleonic grasp of his situation, he reached far and near, hauling this and that dish of fragments towards his plate, giving orders at the same time, and throwing into his cheerful mouth odd pieces of bread and pickles in an unstudied and preliminary manner. When he had secured everything within his reach, he heaped his plate and began an attack upon the contents, using both knife and fork with wonderful proficiency. The man's good-humor was contagious, and he did not regard our amusement as different in kind from his enjoyment. The spectacle was worth a journey to see. Indeed, its aspect of comicality almost overcame its grossness, and even when the hero loaded in faster than he could swallow, and was obliged to drop his knife for an instant to arrange matters in his mouth with his finger, it was done with such a beaming smile that a pig would not take offense at it. The performance was not the merely vulgar thing it seems on paper, but an achievement unique and perfect, which one is not likely to see more than once in a lifetime. It was only when the man left the table that his face became serious. We had seen him at his best.

Prince Edward Island, as we approached it, had a pleasing aspect, and nothing of that remote friendlessness which its appearance on the map conveys to one; a warm and sandy land, in a genial climate, without fogs, we are informed. In the winter it has ice communication with Nova Scotia, from Cape Traverse to Cape Tormentine,--the route of the submarine cable. The island is as flat from end to end as a floor. When it surrendered its independent government and joined the Dominion, one of the conditions of the union was that the government should build a railway the whole length of it. This is in process of construction, and the portion that is built affords great satisfaction to the islanders, a railway being one of the necessary adjuncts of civilization; but that there was great need of it, or that it would pay, we were unable to learn.

We sailed through Hillsborough Bay and a narrow strait to Charlottetown, the capital, which lies on a sandy spit of land between two rivers. Our leisurely steamboat tied up here in the afternoon and spent the night, giving the passengers an opportunity to make thorough acquaintance with the town. It has the appearance of a place from which something has departed; a wooden town, with wide and vacant streets, and the air of waiting for something. Almost melancholy is the aspect of its freestone colonial building, where once the colonial legislature held its momentous sessions, and the colonial governor shed the delightful aroma of royalty. The mansion of the governor--now vacant of pomp, because that official does not exist--is a little withdrawn from the town, secluded among trees by the water-side. It is dignified with a winding approach, but is itself only a cheap and decaying house. On our way to it we passed the drill-shed of the local cavalry, which we mistook for a skating-rink, and thereby excited the contempt of an old lady of whom we inquired. Tasteful residences we did not find, nor that attention to flowers and gardens which the mild climate would suggest. Indeed, we should describe Charlottetown as a place where the hollyhock in the dooryard is considered an ornament. A conspicuous building is a large market-house shingled all over (as many of the public buildings are), and this and other cheap public edifices stand in the midst of a large square, which is surrounded by shabby shops for the most part. The town is laid out on a generous scale, and it is to be regretted that we could not have seen it when it enjoyed the glory of a governor and court and ministers of state, and all the paraphernalia of a royal parliament. That the productive island, with its system of free schools, is about to enter upon a prosperous career, and that Charlottetown is soon to become a place of great activity, no one who converses with the natives can doubt; and I think that even now no traveler will regret spending an hour or two there; but it is necessary to say that the rosy inducements to tourists to spend the summer there exist only in the guide-books.

We congratulated ourselves that we should at least have a night of delightful sleep on the steamboat in the quiet of this secluded harbor. But it was wisely ordered otherwise, to the end that we should improve our time by an interesting study of human nature. Towards midnight, when the occupants of all the staterooms were supposed to be in profound slumber, there was an invasion of the small cabin by a large and loquacious family, who had been making an excursion on the island railway. This family might remind an antiquated novel-reader of the delightful Brangtons in "Evelina;" they had all the vivacity of the pleasant cousins of the heroine of that story, and the same generosity towards the public in regard to their family affairs. Before they had been in the cabin an hour, we felt as if we knew every one of them. There was a great squabble as to where and how they should sleep; and when this was over, the revelations of the nature of their beds and their peculiar habits of sleep continued to pierce the thin deal partitions of the adjoining state-rooms. When all the possible trivialities of vacant minds seemed to have been exhausted, there followed a half-hour of "Goodnight, pa; good-night, ma;" "Goodnight, pet;" and "Are you asleep, ma?" "No." "Are you asleep, pa?" "No; go to sleep, pet." "I'm going. Good-night, pa; good-night, ma." "Goodnight, pet." "This bed is too short." "Why don't you take the other?" "I'm all fixed now." "Well, go to sleep; good-night." "Good-night, ma; goodnight, pa,"--no answer. "Good-night,pa." "Goodnight, pet." "Ma, are you asleep?" "Most." "This bed is all lumps; I wish I'd gone downstairs." "Well, pa will get up." "Pa, are you asleep?" "Yes." "It's better now; good-night, pa." "Goodnight, pet." "Good-night, ma." "Good-night, pet." And so on in an exasperating repetition, until every passenger on the boat must have been thoroughly informed of the manner in which this interesting family habitually settled itself to repose.

Half an hour passes with only a languid exchange of family feeling, and then: "Pa?" "Well, pet." "Don't call us in the morning; we don't want any breakfast; we want to sleep." "I won't." "Goodnight, pa; goodnight, ma. Ma?" "What is it, dear?" "Good-night, ma." "Good-night, pet." Alas for youthful expectations! Pet shared her stateroom with a young companion, and the two were carrying on a private dialogue during this public performance. Did these young ladies, after keeping all the passengers of the boat awake till near the summer dawn, imagine that it was in the power of pa and ma to insure them the coveted forenoon slumber, or even the morning snooze? The travelers, tossing in their state-room under this domestic infliction, anticipated the morning with grim satisfaction; for they had a presentiment that it would be impossible for them to arise and make their toilet without waking up every one in their part of the boat, and aggravating them to such an extent that they would stay awake. And so it turned out. The family grumbling at the unexpected disturbance was sweeter to the travelers than all the exchange of family affection during the night.

No one, indeed, ought to sleep beyond breakfast-time while sailing along the southern coast of Prince Edward Island. It was a sparkling morning. When we went on deck we were abreast Cape Traverse; the faint outline of Nova Scotia was marked on the horizon, and New Brunswick thrust out Cape Tomentine to greet us. On the still, sunny coasts and the placid sea, and in the serene, smiling sky, there was no sign of the coming tempest which was then raging from Hatteras to Cape Cod; nor could one imagine that this peaceful scene would, a few days later, be swept by a fearful tornado, which should raze to the ground trees and dwelling-houses, and strew all these now inviting shores with wrecked ships and drowning sailors,--a storm which has passed into literature in "The Lord's-Day Gale" of Mr Stedman.

Through this delicious weather why should the steamboat hasten, in order to discharge its passengers into the sweeping unrest of continental travel? Our eagerness to get on, indeed, almost melted away, and we were scarcely impatient at all when the boat lounged into Halifax Bay, past Salutation Point and stopped at Summerside. This little seaport is intended to be attractive, and it would give these travelers great pleasure to describe it, if they could at all remember how it looks. But it is a place that, like some faces, makes no sort of impression on the memory. We went ashore there, and tried to take an interest in the ship-building, and in the little oysters which the harbor yields; but whether we did take an interest or not has passed out of memory. A small, unpicturesque, wooden town, in the languor of a provincial summer; why should we pretend an interest in it which we did not feel? It did not disturb our reposeful frame of mind, nor much interfere with our enjoyment of the day.

On the forward deck, when we were under way again, amid a group reading and nodding in the sunshine, we found a pretty girl with a companion and a gentleman, whom we knew by intuition as the "pa" of the pretty girl and of our night of anguish. The pa might have been a clergyman in a small way, or the proprietor of a female boarding-school; at any rate, an excellent and improving person to travel with, whose willingness to impart information made even the travelers long for a pa. It was no part of his plan of this family summer excursion, upon which he had come against his wish, to have any hour of it wasted in idleness. He held an open volume in his hand, and was questioning his daughter on its contents. He spoke in a loud voice, and without heeding the timidity of the young lady, who shrank from this public examination, and begged her father not to continue it. The parent was, however, either proud of his daughter's acquirements, or he thought it a good opportunity to shame her out of her ignorance. Doubtless, we said, he is instructing her upon the geography of the region we are passing through, its early settlement, the romantic incidents of its history when French and English fought over it, and so is making this a tour of profit as well as pleasure. But the excellent and pottering father proved to be no disciple of the new education. Greece was his theme and he got his questions, and his answers too, from the ancient school history in his hand. The lesson went on:

"Who was Alcibiades?

"A Greek."

"Yes. When did he flourish?"

"I can't think."

"Can't think? What was he noted for?"

"I don't remember."

"Don't remember? I don't believe you studied this."

"Yes, I did."

"Well, take it now, and study it hard, and then I'll hear you again."

The young girl, who is put to shame by this open persecution, begins to study, while the peevish and small tyrant, her pa, is nagging her with such soothing remarks as, "I thought you'd have more respect for your pride;" "Why don't you try to come up to the expectations of your teacher?" By and by the student thinks she has "got it," and the public exposition begins again. The date at which Alcibiades "flourished" was ascertained, but what he was "noted for" got hopelessly mixed with what Thernistocles was "noted for." The momentary impression that the battle of Marathon was fought by Salamis was soon dissipated, and the questions continued.

"What did Pericles do to the Greeks?"

"I don't know."

"Elevated 'em, did n't he? Did n't he elevate Pem?"

"Yes, sir."

"Always remember that; you want to fix your mind on leading things. Remember that Pericles elevated the Greeks. Who was Pericles?

"He was a"--

"Was he a philosopher?"

"Yes, sir."

"No, he was n't. Socrates was a philosopher. When did he flourish?"

And so on, and so on.

O my charming young countrywomen, let us never forget that Pericles elevated the Greeks; and that he did it by cultivating the national genius, the national spirit, by stimulating art and oratory and the pursuit of learning, and infusing into all society a higher intellectual and social life! Pa was this day sailing through seas and by shores that had witnessed some of the most stirring and romantic events in the early history of our continent. He might have had the eager attention of his bright daughter if he had unfolded these things to her in the midst of this most living landscape, and given her an "object lesson" that she would not have forgotten all her days, instead of this pottering over names and dates that were as dry and meaningless to him as they were uninteresting to his daughter. At least, O Pa, Educator of Youth, if you are insensible to the beauty of these summer isles and indifferent to their history, and your soul is wedded to ancient learning, why do you not teach your family to go to sleep when they go to bed, as the classic Greeks used to?

Before the travelers reached Shediac, they had leisure to ruminate upon the education of American girls in the schools set apart for them, and to conjecture how much they are taught of the geography and history of America, or of its social and literary growth; and whether, when they travel on a summer tour like this, these coasts have any historical light upon them, or gain any interest from the daring and chivalric adventurers who played their parts here so long ago. We did not hear pa ask when Madame de la Tour "flourished," though "flourish" that determined woman did, in Boston as well as in the French provinces. In the present woman revival, may we not hope that the heroic women of our colonial history will have the prominence that is their right, and that woman's achievements will assume their proper place in affairs? When women write history, some of our popular men heroes will, we trust, be made to acknowledge the female sources of their wisdom and their courage. But at present women do not much affect history, and they are more indifferent to the careers of the noted of their own sex than men are.

We expected to approach Shediac with a great deal of interest. It had been, when we started, one of the most prominent points in our projected tour. It was the pivot upon which, so to speak, we expected to swing around the Provinces. Upon the map it was so attractive, that we once resolved to go no farther than there. It once seemed to us that, if we ever reached it, we should be contented to abide there, in a place so remote, in a port so picturesque and foreign. But returning from the real east, our late interest in Shediac seemed unaccountable to us. Firmly resolved as I was to note our entrance into the harbor, I could not keep the place in mind; and while we were in our state-room and before we knew it, the steamboat Jay at the wharf. Shediac appeared to be nothing but a wharf with a railway train on it, and a few shanty buildings, a part of them devoted to the sale of whiskey and to cheap lodgings. This landing, however, is called Point du Chene, and the village of Shediac is two or three miles distant from it; we had a pleasant glimpse of it from the car windows, and saw nothing in its situation to hinder its growth. The country about it is perfectly level, and stripped of its forests. At Painsec Junction we waited for the train from Halifax, and immediately found ourselves in the whirl of intercolonial travel. Why people should travel here, or why they should be excited about it, we could not see; we could not overcome a feeling of the unreality of the whole thing; but yet we humbly knew that we had no right to be otherwise than awed by the extraordinary intercolonial railway enterprise and by the new life which it is infusing into the Provinces. We are free to say, however, that nothing can be less interesting than the line of this road until it strikes the Kennebeckasis River, when the traveler will be called upon to admire the Sussex Valley and a very fair farming region, which he would like to praise if it were not for exciting the jealousy of the "Garden of Nova Scotia." The whole land is in fact a garden, but differing somewhat from the Isle of Wight.

In all travel, however, people are more interesting than land, and so it was at this time. As twilight shut down upon the valley of the Kennebeckasis, we heard the strident voice of pa going on with the Grecian catechism. Pa was unmoved by the beauties of Sussex or by the colors of the sunset, which for the moment made picturesque the scraggy evergreens on the horizon. His eyes were with his heart, and that was in Sparta. Above the roar of the car-wheels we heard his nagging inquiries.

"What did Lycurgus do then?"

Answer not audible.

"No. He made laws. Who did he make laws for?"

"For the Greeks."

"He made laws for the Lacedemonians. Who was another great lawgiver?"

"It was--it was--Pericles."

"No, it was n't. It was Solon. Who was Solon?"

"Solon was one of the wise men of Greece."

"That's right. When did he flourish?"

When the train stops at a station the classics continue, and the studious group attracts the attention of the passengers. Pa is well pleased, but not so the young lady, who beseechingly says,

"Pa, everybody can hear us."

"You would n't care how much they heard, if you knew it," replies this accomplished devotee of learning.

In another lull of the car-wheels we find that pa has skipped over to Marathon; and this time it is the daughter who is asking a question.

"Pa, what is a phalanx?"

"Well, a phalanx--it's a--it's difficult to define a phalanx. It's a stretch of men in one line,--a stretch of anything in a line. When did Alexander flourish?"

This domestic tyrant had this in common with the rest of us, that he was much better at asking questions than at answering them. It certainly was not our fault that we were listeners to his instructive struggles with ancient history, nor that we heard his petulant complaining to his cowed family, whom he accused of dragging him away on this summer trip. We are only grateful to him, for a more entertaining person the traveler does not often see. It was with regret that we lost sight of him at St. John.

Night has settled upon New Brunswick and upon ancient Greece before we reach the Kennebeckasis Bay, and we only see from the car windows dimly a pleasant and fertile country, and the peaceful homes of thrifty people. While we are running along the valley and coming under the shadow of the hill whereon St. John sits, with a regal outlook upon a most variegated coast and upon the rising and falling of the great tides of Fundy, we feel a twinge of conscience at the injustice the passing traveler must perforce do any land he hurries over and does not study. Here is picturesque St. John, with its couple of centuries of history and tradition, its commerce, its enterprise felt all along the coast and through the settlements of the territory to the northeast, with its no doubt charming society and solid English culture; and the summer tourist, in an idle mood regarding it for a day, says it is naught! Behold what "travels" amount to! Are they not for the most part the records of the misapprehensions of the misinformed? Let us congratulate ourselves that in this flight through the Provinces we have not attempted to do any justice to them, geologically, economically, or historically, only trying to catch some of the salient points of the panorama as it unrolled itself. Will Halifax rise up in judgment against us? We look back upon it with softened memory, and already see it again in the light of history. It stands, indeed, overlooking a gate of the ocean, in a beautiful morning light; and we can hear now the repetition of that profane phrase, used for the misdirection of wayward mortals,---"Go to Halifax!" without a shudder.

We confess to some regret that our journey is so near its end. Perhaps it is the sentimental regret with which one always leaves the east, for we have been a thousand miles nearer Ireland than Boston is. Collecting in the mind the detached pictures given to our eyes in all these brilliant and inspiring days, we realize afresh the variety, the extent, the richness of these northeastern lands which the Gulf Stream pets and tempers. If it were not for attracting speculators, we should delight to speak of the beds of coal, the quarries of marble, the mines of gold. Look on the map and follow the shores of these peninsulas and islands, the bays, the penetrating arms of the sea, the harbors filled with islands, the protected straits and sounds. All this is favorable to the highest commercial activity and enterprise. Greece itself and its islands are not more indented and inviting. Fish swarm about the shores and in all the streams. There are, I have no doubt, great forests which we did not see from the car windows, the inhabitants of which do not show themselves to the travelers at the railway-stations. In the dining-room of a friend, who goes away every autumn into the wilds of Nova Scotia at the season when the snow falls, hang trophies --enormous branching antlers of the caribou, and heads of the mighty moose--which I am assured came from there; and I have no reason to doubt that the noble creatures who once carried these superb horns were murdered by my friend at long range. Many people have an insatiate longing to kill, once in their life, a moose, and would travel far and endure great hardships to gratify this ambition. In the present state of the world it is more difficult to do it than it is to be written down as one who loves his fellow-men.

We received everywhere in the Provinces courtesy and kindness, which were not based upon any expectation that we would invest in mines or railways, for the people are honest, kindly, and hearty by nature. What they will become when the railways are completed that are to bind St. John to Quebec, and make Nova Scotia, Cape Breton, and Newfoundland only stepping-stones to Europe, we cannot say. Probably they will become like the rest of the world, and furnish no material for the kindly persiflage of the traveler.

Regretting that we could see no more of St. John, that we could scarcely see our way through its dimly lighted streets, we found the ferry to Carleton, and a sleeping-car for Bangor. It was in the heart of the negro porter to cause us alarm by the intelligence that the customs officer would, search our baggage during the night. A search is a blow to one's self-respect, especially if one has anything dutiable. But as the porter might be an agent of our government in disguise, we preserved an appearance of philosophical indifference in his presence. It takes a sharp observer to tell innocence from assurance. During the night, awaking, I saw a great light. A man, crawling along the aisle of the car, and poking under the seats, had found my traveling-bag and was "going through" it.

I felt a thrill of pride as I recognized in this crouching figure an officer of our government, and knew that I was in my native land.

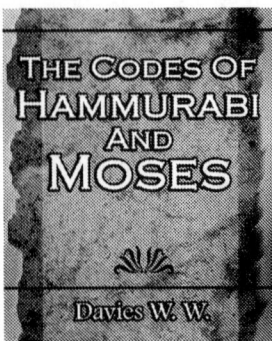

The Codes Of Hammurabi And Moses
W. W. Davies

QTY

The discovery of the Hammurabi Code is one of the greatest achievements of archaeology, and is of paramount interest, not only to the student of the Bible, but also to all those interested in ancient history...

Religion   **ISBN:** *1-59462-338-4*   **Pages:132**
MSRP $12.95

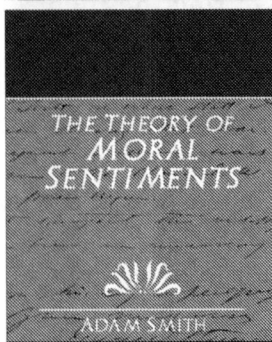

The Theory of Moral Sentiments
Adam Smith

QTY

This work from 1749. contains original theories of conscience amd moral judgment and it is the foundation for systemof morals.

Philosophy   **ISBN:** *1-59462-777-0*   **Pages:536**
MSRP $19.95

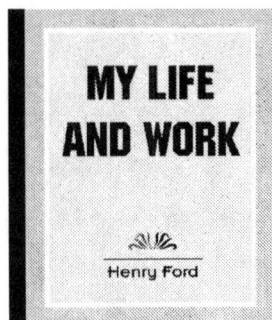

Jessica's First Prayer
Hesba Stretton

QTY

In a screened and secluded corner of one of the many railway-bridges which span the streets of London there could be seen a few years ago, from five o'clock every morning until half past eight, a tidily set-out coffee-stall, consisting of a trestle and board, upon which stood two large tin cans, with a small fire of charcoal burning under each so as to keep the coffee boiling during the early hours of the morning when the work-people were thronging into the city on their way to their daily toil...

Pages:84

Childrens   **ISBN:** *1-59462-373-2*   *MSRP $9.95*

My Life and Work
Henry Ford

QTY

Henry Ford revolutionized the world with his implementation of mass production for the Model T automobile. Gain valuable business insight into his life and work with his own auto-biography... "We have only started on our development of our country we have not as yet, with all our talk of wonderful progress, done more than scratch the surface. The progress has been wonderful enough but..."

Pages:300

Biographies/   **ISBN:** *1-59462-198-5*   *MSRP $21.95*

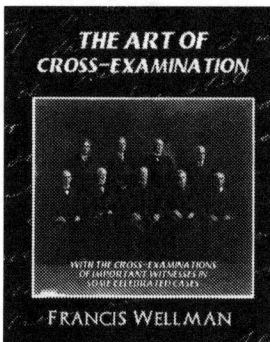

The Art of Cross-Examination
Francis Wellman

QTY

I presume it is the experience of every author, after his first book is published upon an important subject, to be almost overwhelmed with a wealth of ideas and illustrations which could readily have been included in his book, and which to his own mind, at least, seem to make a second edition inevitable. Such certainly was the case with me; and when the first edition had reached its sixth impression in five months, I rejoiced to learn that it seemed to my publishers that the book had met with a sufficiently favorable reception to justify a second and considerably enlarged edition. ..

Reference **ISBN:** *1-59462-647-2*   **Pages:412**
                                        MSRP $19.95

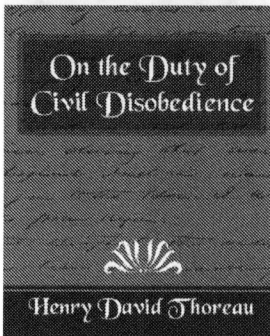

On the Duty of Civil Disobedience
Henry David Thoreau

QTY

Thoreau wrote his famous essay, On the Duty of Civil Disobedience, as a protest against an unjust but popular war and the immoral but popular institution of slave-owning. He did more than write—he declined to pay his taxes, and was hauled off to gaol in consequence. Who can say how much this refusal of his hastened the end of the war and of slavery ?

Law   **ISBN:** *1-59462-747-9*   **Pages:48**
                                        MSRP $7.45

Dream Psychology Psychoanalysis for Beginners
Sigmund Freud

QTY

Sigmund Freud, born Sigismund Schlomo Freud (May 6, 1856 - September 23, 1939), was a Jewish-Austrian neurologist and psychiatrist who co-founded the psychoanalytic school of psychology. Freud is best known for his theories of the unconscious mind, especially involving the mechanism of repression; his redefinition of sexual desire as mobile and directed towards a wide variety of objects; and his therapeutic techniques, especially his understanding of transference in the therapeutic relationship and the presumed value of dreams as sources of insight into unconscious desires.

Psychology **ISBN:** *1-59462-905-6*   **Pages:196**
                                        MSRP $15.45

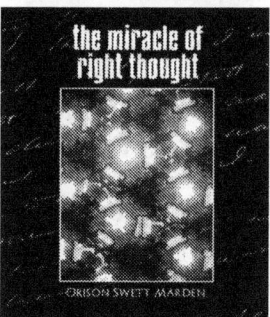

The Miracle of Right Thought
Orison Swett Marden

QTY

Believe with all of your heart that you will do what you were made to do. When the mind has once formed the habit of holding cheerful, happy, prosperous pictures, it will not be easy to form the opposite habit. It does not matter how improbable or how far away this realization may see, or how dark the prospects may be, if we visualize them as best we can, as vividly as possible, hold tenaciously to them and vigorously struggle to attain them, they will gradually become actualized, realized in the life. But a desire, a longing without endeavor, a yearning abandoned or held indifferently will vanish without realization.

Self Help   **ISBN:** *1-59462-644-8*   **Pages:360**
                                        MSRP $25.45

www.bookjungle.com *email: sales@bookjungle.com fax: 630-214-0564 mail: Book Jungle PO Box 2226 Champaign, IL 61825*

QTY

The Rosicrucian Cosmo-Conception Mystic Christianity *by Max Heindel* — ISBN: *1-59462-188-8* **$38.95**
The Rosicrucian Cosmo-conception is not dogmatic, neither does it appeal to any other authority than the reason of the student. It is: not controversial, but is: sent forth in the, hope that it may help to clear.. New Age/Religion Pages 646

Abandonment To Divine Providence *by Jean-Pierre de Caussade* — ISBN: *1-59462-228-0* **$25.95**
"The Rev. Jean Pierre de Caussade was one of the most remarkable spiritual writers of the Society of Jesus in France in the 18th Century. His death took place at Toulouse in 1751. His works have gone through many editions and have been republished... Inspirational/Religion Pages 400

Mental Chemistry *by Charles Haanel* — ISBN: *1-59462-192-6* **$23.95**
Mental Chemistry allows the change of material conditions by combining and appropriately utilizing the power of the mind. Much like applied chemistry creates something new and unique out of careful combinations of chemicals the mastery of mental chemistry... New Age Pages 354

The Letters of Robert Browning and Elizabeth Barret Barrett 1845-1846 vol II — ISBN: *1-59462-193-4* **$35.95**
by Robert Browning and *Elizabeth Barrett* Biographies Pages 596

Gleanings In Genesis (volume I) *by Arthur W. Pink* — ISBN: *1-59462-130-6* **$27.45**
Appropriately has Genesis been termed "the seed plot of the Bible" for in it we have, in germ form, almost all of the great doctrines which are afterwards fully developed in the books of Scripture which follow... Religion/Inspirational Pages 420

The Master Key *by L. W. de Laurence* — ISBN: *1-59462-001-6* **$30.95**
In no branch of human knowledge has there been a more lively increase of the spirit of research during the past few years than in the study of Psychology, Concentration and Mental Discipline. The requests for authentic lessons in Thought Control, Mental Discipline and... New Age/Business Pages 422

The Lesser Key Of Solomon Goetia *by L. W. de Laurence* — ISBN: *1-59462-092-X* **$9.95**
This translation of the first book of the "Lernegton" which is now for the first time made accessible to students of Talismanic Magic was done, after careful collation and edition, from numerous Ancient Manuscripts in Hebrew, Latin, and French... New Age/Occult Pages 92

Rubaiyat Of Omar Khayyam *by Edward Fitzgerald* — ISBN:*1-59462-332-5* **$13.95**
Edward Fitzgerald, whom the world has already learned, in spite of his own efforts to remain within the shadow of anonymity, to look upon as one of the rarest poets of the century, was born at Bredfield, in Suffolk, on the 31st of March, 1809. He was the third son of John Purcell... Music Pages 172

Ancient Law *by Henry Maine* — ISBN: *1-59462-128-4* **$29.95**
The chief object of the following pages is to indicate some of the earliest ideas of mankind, as they are reflected in Ancient Law, and to point out the relation of those ideas to modern thought. Religion/History Pages 452

Far-Away Stories *by William J. Locke* — ISBN: *1-59462-129-2* **$19.45**
"Good wine needs no bush,' but a collection of mixed vintages does. And this book is just such a collection. Some of the stories I do not want to remain buried for ever in the museum files of dead magazine-numbers an author's not unpardonable vanity..." Fiction Pages 272

Life of David Crockett *by David Crockett* — ISBN: *1-59462-250-7* **$27.45**
"Colonel David Crockett was one of the most remarkable men of the times in which he lived. Born in humble life, but gifted with a strong will, an indomitable courage, and unremitting perseverance... Biographies/New Age Pages 424

Lip-Reading *by Edward Nitchie* — ISBN: *1-59462-206-X* **$25.95**
Edward B. Nitchie, founder of the New York School for the Hard of Hearing, now the Nitchie School of Lip-Reading, Inc, wrote "LIP-READING Principles and Practice". The development and perfecting of this meritorious work on lip-reading was an undertaking... How-to Pages 400

A Handbook of Suggestive Therapeutics, Applied Hypnotism, Psychic Science — ISBN: *1-59462-214-0* **$24.95**
by Henry Munro Health/New Age/Health/Self-help Pages 376

A Doll's House: and Two Other Plays *by Henrik Ibsen* — ISBN: *1-59462-112-8* **$19.95**
Henrik Ibsen created this classic when in revolutionary 1848 Rome. Introducing some striking concepts in playwriting for the realist genre, this play has been studied the world over. Fiction/Classics/Plays 308

The Light of Asia *by sir Edwin Arnold* — ISBN: *1-59462-204-3* **$13.95**
In this poetic masterpiece, Edwin Arnold describes the life and teachings of Buddha. The man who was to become known as Buddha to the world was born as Prince Gautama of India but he rejected the worldly riches and abandoned the reigns of power when... Religion/History/Biographies Pages 170

The Complete Works of Guy de Maupassant *by Guy de Maupassant* — ISBN: *1-59462-157-8* **$16.95**
"For days and days, nights and nights, I had dreamed of that first kiss which was to consecrate our engagement, and I knew not on what spot I should put my lips..." Fiction/Classics Pages 240

The Art of Cross-Examination *by Francis L. Wellman* — ISBN: *1-59462-309-0* **$26.95**
Written by a renowned trial lawyer, Wellman imparts his experience and uses case studies to explain how to use psychology to extract desired information through questioning. How-to/Science/Reference Pages 408

Answered or Unanswered? *by Louisa Vaughan* — ISBN: *1-59462-248-5* **$10.95**
Miracles of Faith in China Religion Pages 112

The Edinburgh Lectures on Mental Science (1909) *by Thomas* — ISBN: *1-59462-008-3* **$11.95**
This book contains the substance of a course of lectures recently given by the writer in the Queen Street Hall, Edinburgh. Its purpose is to indicate the Natural Principles governing the relation between Mental Action and Material Conditions... New Age/Psychology Pages 148

Ayesha *by H. Rider Haggard* — ISBN: *1-59462-301-5* **$24.95**
Verily and indeed it is the unexpected that happens! Probably if there was one person upon the earth from whom the Editor of this, and of a certain previous history, did not expect to hear again... Classics Pages 380

Ayala's Angel *by Anthony Trollope* — ISBN: *1-59462-352-X* **$29.95**
The two girls were both pretty, but Lucy who was twenty-one who supposed to be simple and comparatively unattractive, whereas Ayala was credited, as her Bombwhat romantic name might show, with poetic charm and a taste for romance. Ayala when her father died was nineteen... Fiction Pages 484

The American Commonwealth *by James Bryce* — ISBN: *1-59462-286-8* **$34.45**
An interpretation of American democratic political theory. It examines political mechanics and society from the perspective of Scotsman James Bryce Politics Pages 572

Stories of the Pilgrims *by Margaret P. Pumphrey* — ISBN: *1-59462-116-0* **$17.95**
This book explores pilgrims religious oppression in England as well as their escape to Holland and eventual crossing to America on the Mayflower, and their early days in New England... History Pages 268

QTY

The Fasting Cure *by Sinclair Upton*　　　　　　　　　　　ISBN: *1-59462-222-1*　**$13.95**
In the Cosmopolitan Magazine for May, 1910, and in the Contemporary Review (London) for April, 1910, I published an article dealing with my experiences in fasting. I have written a great many magazine articles, but never one which attracted so much attention...　New Age/Self Help/Health Pages 164

□

Hebrew Astrology *by Sepharial*　　　　　　　　　　　ISBN: *1-59462-308-2*　**$13.45**
In these days of advanced thinking it is a matter of common observation that we have left many of the old landmarks behind and that we are now pressing forward to greater heights and to a wider horizon than that which represented the mind-content of our progenitors...　Astrology Pages 144

□

Thought Vibration or The Law of Attraction in the Thought World　ISBN: *1-59462-127-6*　**$12.95**
by William Walker Atkinson　　　　　　　　　　　　　　　　*Psychology/Religion Pages 144*

□

Optimism *by Helen Keller*　　　　　　　　　　　　ISBN: *1-59462-108-X*　**$15.95**
Helen Keller was blind, deaf, and mute since 19 months old, yet famously learned how to overcome these handicaps, communicate with the world, and spread her lectures promoting optimism. An inspiring read for everyone...　Biographies/Inspirational Pages 84

□

Sara Crewe *by Frances Burnett*　　　　　　　　　　ISBN: *1-59462-360-0*　**$9.45**
In the first place, Miss Minchin lived in London. Her home was a large, dull, tall one, in a large, dull square, where all the houses were alike, and all the sparrows were alike, and where all the door-knockers made the same heavy sound...　Childrens/Classic Pages 88

□

The Autobiography of Benjamin Franklin *by Benjamin Franklin*　ISBN: *1-59462-135-7*　**$24.95**
The Autobiography of Benjamin Franklin has probably been more extensively read than any other American historical work, and no other book of its kind has had such ups and downs of fortune. Franklin lived for many years in England, where he was agent...　Biographies/History Pages 332

□

Name	
Email	
Telephone	
Address	
City, State ZIP	

□ **Credit Card**　　　　　□ **Check / Money Order**

Credit Card Number	
Expiration Date	
Signature	

Please Mail to:　Book Jungle
PO Box 2226
Champaign, IL 61825
or Fax to:　　630-214-0564

ORDERING INFORMATION

web: *www.bookjungle.com*
email: *sales@bookjungle.com*
fax: *630-214-0564*
mail: *Book Jungle PO Box 2226 Champaign, IL 61825*
or PayPal *to sales@bookjungle.com*

Please contact us for bulk discounts

DIRECT-ORDER TERMS

**20% Discount if You Order
Two or More Books**
Free Domestic Shipping!
Accepted: Master Card, Visa,
Discover, American Express

www.ingramcontent.com/pod-product-compliance
Lightning Source LLC
LaVergne TN
LVHW081325060426

835511LV00011B/1860